Private Voices

Private Voices

THE DIARIES OF
ELIZABETH GASKELL
AND
SOPHIA HOLLAND

EDITED BY
J. A. V. CHAPPLE AND ANITA WILSON

KEELEUNIVERSITYPRESS

First published in 1996
by Keele University Press
Keele, Staffordshire

© The contributors and KUP

Composed by Keele University Press
and printed by Hartnolls, Bodmin, England

ISBN 1 85331 070 0

Contents

Preface

Nancy S. Weyant identified 35 new editions of Elizabeth Gaskell's works and 345 secondary works in the fifteen years covered by her annotated bibliography of English-language sources, 1976–91. Since then the very favourable reception given to Jenny Uglow's *Elizabeth Gaskell: A Habit of Stories* (1993) has underlined the change in Gaskell's reputation. Once known as little more then the charming author of *Cranford*, she is now regarded as a significant and varied Victorian writer, sensitive to the movement of ideas and feelings in her time. Her works are not as artless as they might sometimes seem.

Complete texts of the primary material on which study of her life and works depends have been unavailable to the general reader – such as the diary that Gaskell kept when her daughters Marianne and Meta were very young – or quite unknown – such as the comparable diary kept by Sophia Holland (wife of her cousin Edward) during the early childhood of Marianne's future husband. They anticipate the diary that Emma Darwin kept of the development of her children from 1852, printed in the fourth volume of the *Correspondence of Charles Darwin*.

In an appendix we also print several documents by other relations, the two longest of which have never been printed in full. They all have a more precise bearing on Gaskell's roles as a mother and as the wife of a Unitarian minister than is to be found in general contextual surveys of the period.

The manuscripts

Elizabeth Gaskell's diary, deposited by Mrs Rosemary Trevor Dabbs in the Brotherton Library of the University of Leeds, is contained in a notebook measuring $4\frac{1}{2} \times 7$ inches, bound in marbled boards with spine and corners in calf. The leaves have marbled edges. Machine-made paper is randomly gathered in twelves, though the first gathering consists of six leaves only, perhaps indicating that some leaves were removed. Some of the gatherings bear the watermark 'HARRIS 1822' in open caps. Less than half the book is used.

It was given the title of 'My Diary' by Clement Shorter, who published a limited edition of fifty copies in 1923, now very rare. We are grateful to J. G. Sharps for information about a proof copy in his possession. The only points to be noted in the present context are Shorter's alterations in the preliminaries: he gives the full names of Brian Thurstan Holland and Miss Florence Evelyn Holland (Marianne's younger children). In the published text we find that he changed his original date from 19 May 1923 to 29 May 1923.

Sophia Holland's unpublished diary, deposited by Mrs Portia Holland in the Brotherton Library, is contained in two little notebooks, measuring $3 \times 4\frac{1}{2}$ inches. The first has a soft blue cover, the second a soft marbled one. The insides of the covers have been used and each has nine pairs of leaves of machine-made paper without watermark, stitched through the middle. They are full of writing. At least one more notebook was formerly in the possession of the family, but Mrs Holland does not know where it is now.

We are most grateful to Mrs Dabbs and Mrs Holland for allowing us access to these diaries and giving us permission to print them. Similarly, we would thank Miss B. Hartas Jackson for material printed in the appendix; also, Mrs Joan Leach, Secretary of the Gaskell Society, for information about the Deane family, and David Holland, whose family Bible has supplied dates previously unknown. Sources of new and revised factual information will be found in a forthcoming book by J. A. V. Chapple on Elizabeth Gaskell's family background and life up to 1832.

The texts

Elizabeth Gaskell's diary is unusually neatly written in a handsome, flowing hand. Sophia Holland's writing is much more informal and would have required a great deal of alteration to make it fit modern norms.

We have retained the character of these diaries by transcribing them in a conservative manner, preserving idiosyncratic spellings and making only very minor changes. Superscript letters have been lowered, some full stops or dashes silently added and single quotation marks used instead of double. Wherever punctuation is ambiguous and paragraphing inadequate, especially in the case of the Holland diary, we have consulted the interests of the reader. Insignificant alterations have been ignored. 'MA' (Marianne Gaskell) has been adopted as standard.

Elizabeth Gaskell's Diary

Critical introduction

Anita Wilson

On 10 March 1835, Elizabeth Gaskell began a diary to record the growth and development of her daughter, Marianne, then six months old.[1] The diary is dedicated to Marianne, 'as a token of her mother's love', and as an opportunity 'to become acquainted with her character in it's [*sic*] earliest form' (p. 50).[2] Never intended for publication, Gaskell's diary was privately printed in 1923, when fifty copies were made available to libraries.[3] As a private and domestic piece of writing, it has not received the scholarly consideration which it deserves. Yet Mrs Gaskell's diary remains of interest on its own merits — as a document of Victorian social history and as a foreshadowing of her development as a novelist. Far from a sentimental relic of Gaskell's early adulthood, her first sustained written work is an insightful and self-revealing account of Victorian womanhood and motherhood, integral to an understanding of her life and work. Gaskell herself seems to have been surprised by the extent to which she wrote about herself in writing about her child. 'I had no idea the journal of my own disposition, & feelings was so intimately connected with that of my little baby ...', her first entry concluded (p. 52).

Gaskell brought a complex and somewhat troubled emotional context to her first experience of motherhood. The early loss of her own mother, when Elizabeth was only thirteen months old, left a vacuum which even her loving aunt and surrogate mother, Hannah Lumb, could not completely fill. Gaskell's letters and diary provide ample evidence of the mutual affection and devotion between herself and her aunt; the young Elizabeth was hardly a Dickensian orphan who grew up emotionally desolate. '[O]n May 1st I lost my best friend', Gaskell wrote in 1837 when Aunt Lumb, whom she called 'my more than mother', died of a paralytic stroke (p. 63). In happier days, shortly before her marriage, Elizabeth had hoped that William Gaskell would be able to see more of 'my darling Aunt Lumb' (*Letters*, no. 1, p. 1). Nevertheless, Gaskell felt the loss of her own mother acutely. 'I think no one but one so unfortunate as to be early motherless can enter into the craving one has after the lost mother', she wrote in a letter of 1849 (*Letters*, no. 614, p. 797). Occasional visits with her father and stepmother in

Chelsea had not been happy; without the consolations of the 'beautiful, grand river' and the kindness of neighbours, she recalled, 'I think my child's heart would have broken' (Letters, no. 616, pp. 797–8).[4] Perhaps Gaskell's most blunt and poignant comment appeared in a letter to Charlotte Brontë's friend Ellen Nussey, whose mother had recently died: 'I never knew what it was to have one' (Letters, no. 385a, p. 891).[5]

The lack of any memories of her mother left a painful gap in Gaskell's personal history, which motivated her to provide a tangible keepsake for her own daughter. When Gaskell received some of her mother's letters, 'the only relics of her that I have', she was profoundly grateful, having 'so often longed for some little thing that had once been hers or been touched by her' (Letters, no. 614, pp. 796–7).[6] She ensured that Marianne would know 'the love and the hope that is bound up in her' (p. 50), even if Marianne's mother should not survive to pass on the diary in person.

Writing about Marianne also helped Gaskell to articulate and explore her own feelings as she adjusted to motherhood. No doubt the diary served as a catharsis; in a letter written a few years later, Gaskell commented that her husband 'won't allow me ever to talk to him about anxieties [concerning the children] while it would be SUCH A RELIEF often' (Letters, no. 16, p. 45).[7] Gaskell's sense of maternal deprivation probably intensified her affection and concern for her own children. In addition, she became a mother at the beginning of an age of transition in child-rearing theories and practices. Her emerging roles as new mother and apprentice writer are mutually illuminating as she recounts her experiences with the challenges, dilemmas, and rewards of Victorian parenthood. In this respect, Gaskell's diary proves an intriguing firsthand document of Victorian social history. Her private voice complements the abundant public discourse of an era which bombarded mothers with advice and exhortations in newly fashionable child-care books and in the periodical press.

The Gaskells were among the first generation of Victorian parents to experience the benefits and burdens of a plethora of prescriptive child-care literature. 'Books do so differ', Mrs Gaskell observed (p. 52) with some consternation, when seeking practical advice as a first-time mother. She had plenty of sources to choose from; publications of the 1830s included J. S. C. Abbott, The Mother at Home, or the Principles of Maternal Duty (1830); Louisa Mary Barwell, Nursery Government (1836); Samuel Smiles, Physical Education, or the Nurture and Management of Children (1838); Thomas Bull, Hints to Mothers (1837); William Cobbett, Advice to Young Men ... on How to be a Father (1829); Isaac Taylor, Home Education (1838); Pye Henry Chavasse, Advice to Mothers (1839); and Melasina Trench, Thoughts of a Parent on Education (1837).

The number and diversity of authors attests to the veritable explosion of interest in child-care literature. All these writers catered to an avid audience which was eager to receive the latest advice on feeding, bathing, dressing, disciplining, and loving their children. Chavasse's book remained in print until 1948, guiding British mothers from the Victorian age until the Second World War. Cobbett's pre-Victorian work was unusual in giving men their due as partners in child-rearing. Although fathers were not ignored in Victorian child-care literature, it was directed primarily to mothers. Barwell's book was intended for nurses, but they took a secondary role to mothers, who were generally recognized as the 'moral guides and physical guardians of their children ...' (Hardyment, p. 62). Nurses were regarded as helpers, not as maternal substitutes.

Samuel Smiles, remembered for his best-seller *Self-Help* (1859), first made his mark as a physician writing about children. The two books were close in spirit if not in subject matter. Smiles's optimistic and methodical philosophy of self-improvement also applied to child-rearing. In *Self-Help*, he would define national progress as 'the sum of individual industry, energy, and uprightness ...' (qtd. in Altick, p. 171). And those stellar qualities began in the nursery, with knowledge of the 'powers ... propensities and faculties' of a child's mind (qtd. in Hardyment, p. 41). What could have more potential than a properly nurtured child?

Thomas Bull, who wrote two very successful books on child care, was also a physician and advocated a structured approach to child care, providing detailed instructions, for example, on how, what, and when to feed babies.[8] Bull's rigorous philosophy was in part a defence against the high rate of infant mortality; mothers who were educated in child care would presumably have a better chance of seeing their children survive. But beyond this laudable goal, Bull offered (or imposed) advice on points far removed from nutrition and health. Even the pictures on a nursery wall were subject to scrutiny, since a 'taste in early life for everything refined and beautiful purifies [the child's] mind, cultivates his intellect, keeps him from low company, and makes him grow up a gentleman' (qtd. in Hardyment, p. 64). A well-regulated aesthetic environment functioned rather like an inoculation against corruption; morality, taste, and class consciousness were neatly packaged.

Gaskell cited two works which she found helpful, both of which were popular during the early Victorian period: Albertine Necker de Saussure's *L'Education progressive* (1828–32) and Andrew Combe's *Principles of Physiology Applied to the Preservation of Health, and to the Improvement of Physical and Mental Education* (1834). Combe's book was first published in Edinburgh and was followed in 1840 by *Treatise on the Physiological and Moral Management of Infants*, which was still in print fifty years later. As the titles suggest, both of Combe's books stressed the link between physical well-being and mental and moral development. The small discomforts of hunger, fatigue, teething, etc., were not occasions to stiffen the child's moral fibre; on the contrary, attending to and preferably preventing these impediments cleared the way for healthy growth in body, mind, and spirit.

With his brother George, whose *The Constitution of Man* had been published in 1828, Andrew Combe was a leading advocate of phrenology, the pseudo-science of interpreting bumps on the skull as indications of intelligence and personality traits. Uglow has noted that phrenology 'appealed particularly to women, because it countered suggestions of mental inequality between the sexes ...' (Uglow, p. 65). Moreover, phrenology gave mothers power; by carefully observing a child's temperament, they could supposedly influence his or her traits in a positive direction.

Although Gaskell had visited Edinburgh in the early 1830s and was familiar with phrenology, she was sceptical. In 1831, she gave her friend Harriet Carr a phrenological self-analysis, tongue in cheek: '... I have the organ of causality, alias the reasoning faculty, so very strongly developed, and you know what a reasonable person I am' (to Harriet Carr, 31 August/1 September 1831; qtd. in Uglow, p. 65). Phrenology aside, a few years later Gaskell found that Combe's analysis of the interaction between mind and body confirmed her observations of Marianne's temperament, and of her own 'irritable state of excitement' when lacking sleep or food (p. 55).

Gaskell did not divine Marianne's character by reading the bumps on her head, but she did credit Combe as a trustworthy guide to the 'little freaks of temper' which could mystify an inexperienced mother: 'It is quite astonishing to see the difference bodily feelings make in Marianne's temper & powers of endurance. I was in a great measure prepared for this by Combe's Physiology, but I had no idea how every change of temper might be deduced from some corresponding change in the body' (p. 55). Preventable physical stimuli which in turn led to mental irritation or agitation 'should be avoided', Gaskell concluded, 'with as much care as we would avoid anything moral tending to produce moral evil' (p. 55). As Sharps has pointed out, the analysis of social problems which Gaskell would later convey in her novels was consistent with these early, personal observations of a cause–effect relationship between environment and mental state (Sharps, p. 19).

While Gaskell found Combe's book very useful, her diary suggests that de Saussure may have been closer to her heart as an authority who was also a mother. De Saussure combined empathy with systematic study of child development, based upon observations of her own children. Her recommendation that mothers keep diaries recording their children's maturation may well have inspired Gaskell to follow suit.[9]

L'Education progressive received Gaskell's accolade as 'the nicest book I have read on the subject [of child care] ...' (p. 52). Mary Clarke Mohl, who would become a close friend of Gaskell's in later years, recommended *L'Education progressive* to Elizabeth Reid, the founder of Bedford College for Women.[10] This was not de Saussure's first book; she had written a biography of her more famous cousin, Madame de Staël, which Maria Edgeworth declared had 'too many words and too few anecdotes ...' (letter to Mrs Edgeworth, 10 August 1820, qtd. in Colvin, p. 210).[11] When the two writers met in Switzerland in 1820, Edgeworth gave the woman a more favourable review than the biography: 'Her conversation and manners are quite free from the pomposity and *preparation* which appear in the style of that book' (letter to Sophy Ruxton, 26 September 1820, qtd. in Colvin, p. 252).[12]

Born in 1766, de Saussure was in her sixties when *L'Education progressive* was published. The book's subtitle, *étude du cours de la vie*, attests to her original intention to study moral development, her major interest, throughout the lifespan. Although this ambitious project did not materialize, de Saussure's two volumes gave a remarkably astute analysis of the first three years of life. Her own maternal experience was pre-Victorian, but her advice was thoroughly compatible with the Victorians' faith in laws and systems as the cornerstones of sensible child-rearing:'... in the constancy of the phenomena presented to our view by infancy, the effect of general laws was perceptible' (qtd. in Hardyment, p. 38). Such formidable statements were leavened by warmth and compassion, which made de Saussure's book 'user-friendly' for anxious mothers like the young Elizabeth Gaskell. De Saussure did not lightly disregard the tears of infancy, nor did she follow her countryman Rousseau's advice to toughen children with irregular meals and the notorious cold bath.

De Saussure was firm, however, about the necessity of parental authority. Rousseau's ideal child, in the eponymous *Émile* (1762), was to learn only from experience and to have no sense of obedience. Émile was an abstraction; Rousseau had farmed out his five illegitimate children and had never really been an active parent. De Saussure's own maternal experience had convinced her that Rousseau's philosophy violated parents' deepest instincts and was utterly impractical: 'Perhaps Rousseau has made you uneasy as to the lawfulness of your authority. But if your child be exposed to a real danger, or even a trifling or imaginary inconvenience, you snatch him up in your arms and carry him away; your scruples, your resolution, your theories are all forgotten' (qtd. in Hardyment, p. 80). Might de Saussure have been thinking of her daughter, who died in a fire in 1815? Certainly Gaskell, who worried constantly about Marianne's health and safety, would have appreciated the urgency of this passage.

An avalanche of supposedly authoritative child-rearing literature exerted considerable pressure upon parents, particularly mothers. The first page of Gaskell's diary described her 'extreme anxiety in the formation of her little daughter's character'. There was no time to be lost in moulding a child's future; when Marianne was an infant, Mrs Gaskell eagerly sought principles *'now* which can be carried on through the whole of her education' (p. 52). No longer was it sufficient to 'keep the child clean and sweet, to tumble it and toss it about a good deal, play with it, and keep it in good humour', as William Cadogan, a physician, had recommended in the eighteenth century (qtd. in Hardyment, p. 34). Gaskell's diary does not hark back to this casual and uncomplicated approach, but anticipates the best-selling advice of Sarah Ellis, who warned mothers that a baby's mind was 'deriving nourishment, either of a healthy or unhealthy nature, from everything around it' (Ellis, p. 14). It is not surprising that Mrs Gaskell asked her infant's forgiveness in advance for any maternal errors: '... if when you read this, you trace back any evil, or unhappy feeling to my mismanagement in your childhood forgive me, love!' (p. 50).[13]

'Management' had become a key word in Victorian child-rearing, and 'mismanagement' was a cardinal sin. '[I]n every little case it is so difficult for an undecided person like me to determine at once', Gaskell agonized, 'and yet *every body* & every book says that decision is of such consequence ... that it is almost better for *the time*, to go on with a treatment that is *not bad*, rather than by changing to a better, let the child see your wavering' (p. 54). To love one's children was not, in itself, an adequate foundation for parenthood. Mothers especially were cautioned, by female as well as male writers, against excesses of affection. Mrs Ellis urged mothers to look beyond the delights of 'a fondly-treasured infant ... the amusements of the nursery, and ... the first caresses of childhood ...' (Ellis, p. 14). In *Maternal Management of Children*, Thomas Bull used rather mixed metaphors to illustrate the perils of rampant mother-love: 'Tender human feelings are as useless as the blind caresses that cause animals to strangle their own young without the knowledge that we assume a gardener must have of plants' (qtd. in Hardyment, p. 44). Raising a child was no longer considered a matter of common sense or a natural art acquired through informal advice and personal experience. Without maternal management, maternal love was potentially destructive.

The concept of managing children according to a systematic set of principles prescribed by authorities was part of a constellation of social practices which evolved in the 1830s and 1840s. Etiquette manuals prescribed similarly detailed rules for social rituals, such as 'the way [calling] cards were to be left, the official timetable for visiting, the duration and content of calls ...' (Langland, p. 293). The etiquette book, like the child-care manual, emerged as a socially significant discourse in early Victorian England and was directed primarily to women of the middle class. Elizabeth Langland has discussed the power which these guidebooks to Victorian social practices conferred upon women by making them managers of the ever more subtle and intricate signifiers which denoted a family's social status.

In an analogous fashion, child-care books burdened mothers with perfectionist expectations and a concomitant fear of failure, while also offering a socially sanctioned arena for female ambition and achievement. A particularly striking example, *Mothers of the Wise and Good, with Select Essays on Maternal Duties and Influence*, by Jabez Burns, ran through four editions in 1846. Burns inspired mothers with stories of famous men who supposedly owed everything to maternal influence during their earliest years (Hardyment, p. 35). As the Reverend John C. Abbott declared in another popular work, *The Mother at Home, or the Principles of Maternal Duty*, 'Washington might have been the licentious profligate, and Byron the exemplar of virtue ...' if each had had the other's mother (qtd. in Hardyment, pp. 35–6).

Social constructs of femininity, however, placed limits upon maternal power and conveyed mixed messages to mothers, giving with one hand and taking away with the other. Mothers were entitled to be shrewd and self-assertive; fragility and frivolity had no place in the nursery. Sarah Ellis advised mothers not to be 'so fastidious, so guilty of false delicacy' as to omit themselves in teaching their children gratitude (Ellis, p. 68). Motherhood not only permitted but required the exercise of intelligence; praise and reproof were 'legitimate instruments capable of being used with the most beneficial effect by a judicious woman' (Ellis, p. 77). But Ellis stepped back from granting women either the kind or the degree of power which could undermine their feminine nature, as constructed by Victorian norms. She was careful to point out that good mothers did not exercise authority, but rather sympathy and influence, 'the great secret of woman's power in her social and domestic character'; women's supposedly natural weakness made them 'wholly unfit for wielding the weapon of authority to any useful purpose' (Ellis, p. 28). Ellis's rhetoric encodes masculine and feminine spheres of power. Men wield weapons; women possess a subtle, personalized influence which is equally potent, but construed so as not to threaten essential ideas of masculinity and femininity.

The abundance of child-care literature also confronted mothers with conflicting advice. They had to beware of the Scylla and Charybdis which lurked in every small decision of daily life. For instance, should the baby's bath water be warm or cold? Bull argued that discomforts from physical care provided moral lessons in patience. William and Anne Cobbett had sung at full volume to drown out their children's wails during salubrious cold baths. De Saussure, on the other hand, interpreted such distress as a signal to refrain from subjecting children to the miseries of chilly water. On one point the experts were united; everything had consequences for a child's health and character. Nothing was too minor to worry about or too trivial to put to good use.

Gaskell gives a perceptive account of herself as a conscientious and well-informed Victorian mother who tried to synthesize dictums from the nineteenth-century equivalents of Dr Spock with her own day-to-day experiences and observations. For example, she was unsure whether to follow the Draconian philosophy in one unidentified source, 'Do not let [children] have anything they cry for', or to take the gentler approach advocated by de Saussure. 'So I had to make a rule for myself, and ... I still think it a good one', Gaskell stated with apparent satisfaction (p. 52). She concluded that since crying is a baby's only means of communication, it should not become a disciplinary issue unless the child demanded something which she should not have. Otherwise, Gaskell saw no point in trying the child's patience unnecessarily. She likewise rejected 'the plan in fashion formerly, of *making* trials for young children', as a means of enforcing discipline or building character (p. 55).[14] Instead, Gaskell sought to build a relationship with Marianne based upon mutual affection, trust, and respect. '[A] trustful spirit on her part can not be made by violence, but will come naturally when she sees that we are scrupulous in respecting her little rights', Gaskell commented when Marianne was fifteen months old (p. 58). Ideally, such a relationship would form the basis of internalized discipline, which would eliminate the need for autocratic parenting or severe punishments. 'Oh may this indeed be the beginning of self-government!' Gaskell rejoiced when Marianne, barely a year old, tried not to cry while being bathed (p. 57). But moral rigour had its limits; Gaskell encouraged Marianne by using a thermometer to keep the bath water comfortable.

The foundation of internalized discipline, namely the emotional attachment between parent and child, was deliberately cultivated to ensure that children would absorb parental authority and values along with parental love. Richard Brodhead has described the dynamics of such 'disciplinary intimacy' as follows: '... the child imbibes what the parent stands for in a moral sense along with the parent's physical intimacy and affection' (Brodhead, p. 72). When Marianne was impatient or disobedient, her parents deliberately 'look[ed] grave (not angry)' (p. 57). Anger would undermine the vital bond of trust and affection; the child's motivation for obedience would be based upon fear rather than the desire to please beloved parents. When Marianne behaved well, her parents rewarded her with 'pleased countenances and expressions' and played with her (p. 62). At age two, she spoke of making 'Papa and Mama happy' by being good and making them 'so sorry' when she misbehaved. Talking about the consequences of her behaviour was an important step in her internalizing of parental expectations. Mrs Gaskell considered that her daughter had 'a pretty correct idea as to whether actions are right or wrong' – quite an accomplishment for a toddler, and reassuring evidence that her parents' efforts had been successful (p. 61). By the age of four, Marianne was ready to take another step toward reliance upon internal discipline; Mrs Gaskell tried 'to exercise her conscience by occasionally leaving her to judge if ... an action be right or not' (p. 69).

The Gaskells were probably typical of Victorian parents in their earnest but gentle efforts to develop their child's conscience and self-discipline. 'Parents definitely wished for obedient children ... but controlling children through fear was not condoned', Linda Pollock concluded in her historical study (Pollock, p. 166). Humanitarian reforms in prisons, asylums, and hospitals served to discourage corporal punishment (Taylor, p. 435), while nineteenth-century religious revivals encouraged an emphasis upon conscience rather than externally imposed discipline in child-rearing.[15] 'Let [the child] distinctly feel in himself the difference between obedience and disobedience', recommended one of Mrs Gaskell's contemporaries, Mary Sewell (pp. 105, qtd. in Pollock).[16] Harsh measures were regarded not only as cruel but as ineffectual.

Writing during the same time period as Mrs Gaskell, Sara Coleridge suggested that beating or humiliating a child merely exercised an 'external force which does not touch the heart' (I, pp. 140–1, qtd. in Pollock).[17] The secret of a mother's power and influence, according to Mrs Ellis, was sympathy, not fear. Madame de Saussure likewise urged parents to cultivate 'the favourable season of sympathy' when their children were young; neglect would produce children who understood parents' directives well enough, but who lacked the emotional motivation to please their parents by obeying (qtd. in Hardyment, p. 84). It was not adequate simply to teach children to follow orders. The bond of sympathy would gently lead the child 'to prefer the approbation of its mother, to the gratification of its own appetite' – the basis for discipline without punishment (Ellis, p. 57).

As Michel Foucault has argued in *Discipline and Punish*, the subtlety of such non-physical approaches to discipline could exert a more deeply rooted form of control than corporal punishment. The psyche, rather than the body, became the locus of discipline, and the parents' love became inseparable from their authority.[18] Consequently, liberation from severe punishments did not necessarily give Victorian children greater freedom than their predecessors. Mrs Gaskell's early Victorian diary provides an interesting comparison with the memoirs of Elizabeth Grant, who was born in 1797 and recalled her childhood as a curious mixture of barbaric discipline and exhilarating freedom. When the Grant children could not eat foods which made them ill, their father accompanied them to meals with a whip, which he applied liberally. Grant's younger sister was denied food for thirty hours when she would not eat the spinach which she could not digest. 'The dungeons of feudal times were in their degree not more iniquitous than these proceedings', Grant declared with righteous indignation (qtd. in Pollock, pp. 58–9), and no doubt Elizabeth Gaskell and Sarah Ellis would have agreed. Yet there were compensations for what Grant called the dark side of her childhood; 'despotically as we were ruled in some respects, we were left in other ways to our own devices', she recalled (qtd. in Pollock, p. 60).[19] Discipline was brutal, but its scope and duration were limited.

In contrast, Victorian parents attempted to monitor their children, both externally, through careful supervision, and internally, by instilling a sensitive conscience which was attuned to parental expectations. How the child felt about his or her conduct was as important as the behaviour itself. '[I]s Baby sorry for having been impatient[?]' the Gaskells asked their toddler (p. 57). Emotion was a valuable resource for parents' benign manipulation. '[W]hatever we can be made feelingly to comprehend, we distinctly remember …', Mrs Ellis declared (Ellis, p. 44). In effect, parental authority resided within the child, a compelling and pervasive presence. 'When loved parents are properly enshrined in the sanctuary of the mind', Brodhead observed, 'no space is out of their sight …' (Brodhead, pp. 72–3).

The issue of corporal punishment remained problematic for Victorian parents; what was one to do when gentler forms of child management had failed? Since cultural expectations were very high both for children and parents, there was little room for error; Mrs Gaskell was worried about her daughter's 'obstinacy' when Marianne was six months old. Another 'Young

Mother' wrote to a magazine for advice on obtaining 'prompt obedience without too much severity' from children aged one to three years (qtd. in Branca, p. 110). If such a recipe existed, it continued to elude child-care authors as well as parents. Mrs Gaskell noted with regret that it was '*most difficult to find a judicious remedy*' when Marianne refused to co-operate with her parents' noble efforts (p. 68). A few years later, Mrs Ellis condemned 'those horrible whippings of former times', but simultaneously urged mothers to exercise 'unyielding authority' (Ellis, pp. 20, 22). Conscientious parents like the Gaskells not infrequently found themselves in a double bind – if they allowed a child too much leeway, they were bad parents, but if they resorted to harsh methods of enforcing obedience, they had likewise failed. Mrs Gaskell's diary illustrates this dilemma very well. Three-year-old Marianne refused to say the letter 'A' one evening when her parents were teaching her the alphabet: '[S]o Wm gave her a slap on her hand every time she refused to say it, till at last she said it quite pat. Still I am sure we were so unhappy that we cried, when she was gone to bed. And I don't know if it was right. If not pray, dear Marianne, forgive us' (p. 65). Marianne was not punished for failure in her reading lesson; Gaskell makes clear that she knew her letters and that, in any case, the lessons were intended more as a pastime during long winter evenings than as formal instruction. According to Mrs Gaskell, this was the only occasion when Marianne received a 'severe punishment' (p. 65). The principle of obedience was at stake, although the incident itself was trivial. Nevertheless, the Gaskells could not assuage their anguish with the old certitude of 'spare the rod and spoil the child'. That Marianne will eventually be the judge of her parents' conduct shows the new primacy of the child.[20]

It is tempting to speculate that as William Gaskell's paternal role expanded, discipline became more severe, with Elizabeth Gaskell perhaps a reluctant accomplice rather than a partner. Lynn Woodbury's study of Mrs Gaskell's early career suggests that she taught her daughter the '"habits of obedience" required of women in a male-dominated society'. The diary does indicate that William became more directly involved in his daughter's upbringing as she matured; in the entries following Marianne's infancy, Mrs Gaskell writes more frequently of what 'we' thought or did concerning the child. She also indicates that Marianne had a good and affectionate relationship with her father from a very early age. 'She is extremely fond of her Papa, shouting out his name whenever she hears his footstep, never mistaking it ...', Mrs Gaskell wrote when Marianne was fifteen months old (p. 58). And William Gaskell's misery after giving his child a few slaps on the hand hardly fits the stereotype of the stern Victorian paterfamilias.[21] The 'habits of obedience' which both parents enforced, at the cost of some pain to themselves as well as to Marianne, were integral to Mrs Gaskell's own convictions, rather than a regimen imposed by her husband. The Gaskells' shared Unitarian faith emphasized the importance of an individual's reasoning and personal conscience, but such freedom required self-discipline in order to be exercised wisely. The diary as a whole suggests that the Gaskells sought not to extinguish their daughter's self-assertion but to discipline and channel it.

The Gaskells apparently agreed upon the principles of Marianne's early education, although Mrs Gaskell, like most middle-class Victorian mothers, did most of the actual teaching. From the beginning, the Gaskells chose to let Marianne develop at her own pace, at first physically, and later intellectually and spiritually. '[I] am not very anxious for her to walk or talk earlier than her nature prompts, and as her Papa thinks the same, we allow her to take her own way', Mrs Gaskell wrote shortly before her daughter's first birthday (p. 53). Likewise, lessons a few years later would be 'in compliance with her own wish to learn, which wish I must try to excite' (p. 61). Gaskell hoped to motivate her child but did not seek to exert pressure for precocious development. A medical opinion that overstimulation of young children could result in brain inflammation was cited as confirming the course which the Gaskells had already set.

The first step in Marianne's intellectual growth was to encourage her powers of observation and concentration. 'My object is to give her a habit of fixing her attention', Gaskell explained when Marianne was almost six months old (p. 51). She did not impose upon the baby, but took advantage of opportunities to reinforce Marianne's own reactions. '[W]hen I see her looking very intently at anything', Gaskell reported, 'I take her to it, and let her exercise all her senses upon it – even to tasting, if I am sure it can do her no harm' (p. 51). At twelve months, Marianne was 'remarkably observing' and watched whatever was going on around her with 'continued attention' (p. 56). Such behaviour is typical for a child of Marianne's age; what makes it interesting is the context which Gaskell provides. She valued her daughter's quiet awareness and was careful to distinguish it from mere passivity: 'She is very *feminine* I think in her quietness which is as far removed from inactivity of mind as possible' (p. 56). This is an intriguing synthesis of a traditional feminine quality with the power of mental activity – and it took another observant female to perceive this subtlety. At the tender age of one year, Marianne had become her mother's first character study.

A disconcerting incident which took place a year later illustrates the extent to which Gaskell valued Marianne's increasing ability to observe the life around her. A woman whom Gaskell does not identify did or said something inappropriate, in anger, when Marianne was present. '[T]hat *was* naughty', Marianne remarked the next day. Gaskell found herself in a bind between acknowledging the truth of Marianne's observation and 'preserving her love and respect for the person to whom I allude …' (presumably someone whom Marianne would see again). Gaskell softened the incident by telling Marianne that the grown-up miscreant was very sorry, but she placed truth above respect and social propriety. '[I] knew it was my duty not to weaken her power of discriminating …', Gaskell concluded (p. 62).

Like other episodes in the diary, this incident reveals a vital aspect of Gaskell's own character, which was probably intensified by her maternal role. Telling the truth as she perceived it was a cornerstone of her credo as a novelist, and in later years she paid the price for honesty in controversy and personal anguish. Shortly after her novel *Ruth*, which portrayed an unmarried mother, had been published in 1853, Gaskell commented that she expected readers who disagreed with her choice of a topic 'to be disgusted at the plainness with which in one or two places I have spoken out a small part of what was in my mind' (*Letters*, no. 154, p. 227). It is enlightening to see how, in a seemingly trivial incident seventeen years earlier, Gaskell had gone against social convention to grant her very young daughter the same right to speak her mind.

As Marianne continued to mature, the development of her moral character took priority over academic accomplishments. After the dramatic episode of Marianne's ABCs, which was evidently more traumatic for the parents than for the child, lessons were suspended for a few weeks until she again showed interest. A few months later, the diary announced 'a new era' in Marianne's life. Now aged three and a half, she would begin attending half-day sessions at the local infant school. The Gaskells hoped that Marianne's school would exert a good moral influence, not serve as a goad to precocious learning. '[O]ur reasons for wishing her to go to school', Mrs Gaskell noted, were 'not to advance her rapidly in any branch of learning, for William and I agree in not caring for this; but to perfect her habits of obedience, to give her an idea of conquering difficulties by perseverance; and to make her apply steadily for a short time' (p. 67).

The diary does not include any further account of Marianne's first school experience, but seven months later the moral report card was mixed. On the positive side, Gaskell found Marianne's 'temper and habits of obedience' (p. 69) much improved. By her fourth birthday, Marianne had also begun informal reading and sewing lessons with her mother and was making satisfactory progress. However, Gaskell was concerned and perhaps frustrated by the child's 'want of perseverance and dependance [*sic*] upon others as to her occupations and amusements' (p. 70). Passive compliance was not Mrs Gaskell's aspiration for her daughter. As Marianne overcame the obstinacy of her toddler years and learned to take direction and accept discipline, Gaskell hoped that she would begin to make simple decisions and to take some initiative in everyday activities. In short, she wanted Marianne to learn to think.

A letter written in 1850, when Marianne was sixteen and about to begin boarding school in London, reveals Gaskell's continuing concern for her daughter's intellectual development and her refusal to adhere to conventional notions of ladylike education. Gaskell had received rigorous schooling during her own adolescence, and she was determined that Marianne make the most of her ability for music. Unfortunately, this talent was accompanied by a character flaw which had been evident during Marianne's childhood: 'a certain degree of indolence of mind, which made her unwilling to think hard and long about anything ...' (*Letters*, no. 86, p. 138). Gaskell insisted upon lessons in harmony, to enhance Marianne's power of concentration. She wanted her daughter to understand the principles of music, not merely to receive training for pretty performances. Consequently, Gaskell rejected a school whose accomplishments were limited to 'sweet gentle manners, ladylike deportment and dress, and good regulation of the temper; all excellent things as far as they go', she concluded wryly (*Letters*, no. 86, p. 138). But these fine qualities did not go far enough. Gaskell's priorities for her daughter at age four had been very similar. Good behaviour was certainly desirable, but as a foundation for moral and intellectual growth, not as an end in itself.

Gaskell's diary is perhaps most self-revealing when she writes about the spiritual dimension of motherhood. As the wife of a Unitarian minister, she felt a special responsibility to nurture and safeguard her child's faith. Many years later, she described her sense of God 'being above all in His great peace and wisdom, and yet loving me with an individual love tenderer than any mother's' (*Letters*, no. 223, p. 327). The image of maternal love is poignant, especially considering Gaskell's early loss of her own mother. It also suggests that Gaskell sought to represent divine love to her children through the medium of human love. Like many Victorian mothers, she perceived her maternal role as a sacred trust and a solemn duty. The diary indicates that Gaskell was acutely conscious of her own supposed inadequacies and spiritual shortcomings. She referred to anger as the '"sin that doth so easily beset me,"' and worried that her occasional lapses of patience 'might injure the precious soul which [God] hast given to this little child' (p. 60). The experience of motherhood could bring out real or imagined flaws of character which challenged Gaskell's view of herself. 'William told me the other day I was not of a jealous disposition; I do not think he knows me', Gaskell mused, after she understandably felt hurt when Marianne once showed a preference for her nurse's company instead of her mother's (p. 56). Gaskell may have been overly scrupulous in examining her own character; nevertheless, her observations reveal the sharp impact of maternity upon her self-concept and her conscience.

Nowhere in Gaskell's diary is her spiritual self-scrutiny more intense than in her anguished accounts of Marianne's precarious health. '... I sometimes think I may find this little journal a great help in recalling the memory of my darling child, if we should lose her', she wrote when her daughter was a year and a half old (p. 59). The act of memorializing her child in writing provided some consolation in the face of overwhelming fear. However, Gaskell also prayed that she would not make Marianne 'too much my idol' (p. 57).[22] Even maternal love must submit to the divine will, but the prospect of surrendering her child to God 'without a murmur' was daunting, to say the least. Gaskell's efforts to achieve spiritual obedience and self-discipline provide an interesting parallel to her attempts to teach Marianne 'self-government'.

Prayers for guidance and forgiveness, as well as fervent expressions of gratitude, are recorded throughout the diary. 'I did so try to be resigned; but I
cannot tell how I sickened at my heart ...', Gaskell recalled after Marianne,
in infancy, had been seriously ill (p. 53). Two months later, Gaskell eloquently
summed up the conflict between her profound desire to trust in God and
her boundless love for her child: 'Oh may I try not to fasten & centre my
affections too strongly on such a frail little treasure, but all my anxiety though
it renders me so aware of her fragility of life makes me cling daily more &
more to her' (p. 55).

The fear of loss was not theoretical; a friend's son fell ill with croup on
the same night as Marianne and died a few days later.[23] Accounts by other
Victorian mothers testify to the sad commonality of anxiety too often confirmed in grief. Mary Timms, a contemporary of Elizabeth Gaskell, although
not a personal acquaintance, was also the wife of a minister and kept a diary,
which apparently helped her through a spiritual crisis when her two-year-
old daughter died in 1836. Timms's account progressed from devastation to
an obligatory acceptance ('I know it is my duty ... to be resigned') before
achieving a fervent sense of consolation which perpetuated the mother–
child bond. The dead child could become her mother's guardian angel – 'O
delightful thought!' (pp. 87–8, qtd. in Pollock).[24] And Mrs Gaskell, whose
first child was stillborn, could certainly have identified with Sara Coleridge's
sentiment after the death of a newborn daughter: '... strange as it may seem,
these little speechless creatures ... do twine themselves around a parent's
heart from the hour of their birth' (I, pp. 243–4, qtd. in Pollock).[25]

Ironically, the delicate child whose illnesses prompted such paroxysms of
worry turned out to be the longest lived of the Gaskell children, surviving
her three younger sisters and dying in 1920 at the age of 85. However, Mrs
Gaskell did suffer the death of a child when her son, Willie, died of scarlet
fever in 1845, at the age of ten months. Gaskell's letters concerning her son's
death seem relatively tranquil and resigned in comparison to the anguish
expressed in the diary about Marianne. Possibly the presence of three daughters needing her love and attention, and the birth of a fourth daughter a
year after Willie's death, provided some consolation and forced Gaskell to
turn her mind away from grief.[26] Moreover, her diary was a private document;
even letters to close friends might reflect some deliberate or unconscious
censorship of devastating emotions. In any case, when Gaskell had to face
the ultimate loss which had haunted her with anticipatory anxiety, she felt
it keenly and coped resourcefully – perhaps better than she had imagined
during her early days of motherhood. With her husband's encouragement,
she began writing her first novel, *Mary Barton*. Her religious faith did not
appear to be shaken by her son's death, although she confessed to feeling
'sorely puzzled' and longed to be with her child in the afterlife. But she
resolutely brought herself down to earth. '[I] must not waste my strength
or my time about the never ending sorrow', she wrote to her friend Eliza

Fox. In the same letter, Gaskell regretted that the 'bustling life' which may have been therapeutic also made it difficult 'calmly and bravely to face a great grief, and to view it on every side as to bring the harmony out of it' (*Letters*, no. 70, p. 111). The lasting impact of her son's death was expressed in a terse statement to another friend and correspondent, Anne Shaen: 'That wound will never heal on earth, although hardly any one knows how it has changed me' (*Letters*, no. 25a, p. 57).

However, this sorrow was still some years in the future, as Gaskell continued to confide her hopes and worries to the pages of her diary, a good outlet for what she termed 'Mother's fears'. Along with her own dark night of the soul, Gaskell reflected upon Marianne's developing awareness of religion. The tone of Gaskell's narrative concerning Marianne's religious education is considerably calmer than her intense outpourings when writing about her own inner conflicts and private anxieties. Presumably Gaskell took care not to impose her spiritual tension upon her child. Nor was Marianne pressured to become a paragon of piety, like the sanctimonious clergyman's son in *Jane Eyre,* who wished to 'be a little angel here below' and earned gingerbread by reciting psalms. When Marianne was three years old, Gaskell reported that she had 'never asked any question whatever that could lead to any, even the most simple truths, of religion' (p. 66). The emphatic statement conveys a hint of frustration with Marianne's dilatory progress, but Gaskell confined her role to one of watchfulness for signs of incipient interest.

In the next entry, several months later, Gaskell and her daughter had begun 'to talk together about religion' (p. 67). The choice of words implies an interaction between mother and child rather than lessons imposed from above. After perplexing her mother with such enigmas of theology as when God went to bed, Marianne began to acquire a concept of God which emphasized love and protection rather than fear. There were no fire and brimstone sermons in this Unitarian household. The Gaskells hoped that Marianne's love and desire to please them would 'lead into a higher feeling' of religious sensibility (p. 62). The cornerstones of internalized discipline, trust and intimacy, were also the foundation of religious education, placing the child's familial and spiritual experiences in a similar affective context.

The gentle approach to Marianne's religious education is consistent with the overall picture that Mrs Gaskell gives of her daughter's early upbringing. Gaskell's diary challenges prevalent and persistent stereotypes of stern Victorian families whose repressed children haplessly awaited the insights of modern psychology. In fact, it may well provide a more accurate picture of middle-class Victorian family life than the widely disseminated memoirs of adults who had been mistreated as children and whose painful experiences are too often assumed to be representative of Victorian childhood. Samuel Butler gave a memorable portrait of his sadistic clergyman father in *The Way of All Flesh.* Augustus Hare's childhood memories were equally grim; in one bizarre incident, his pet cat was destroyed because he had become too attached to it. Mary Haldane, born a few years before Marianne Gaskell, recalled being 'shut up for a day at a time and fed only on bread and water' (pp. 43–4, qtd. in Pollock).[27] Accounts of child abuse within Victorian families are undoubtedly significant. However, surveys of public and personal documents concerning Victorian child-rearing suggest that images of cruel parents and brutal punishments may have been overemphasized, creating a distorted picture. In her historical study of child-rearing and family life, Christina Hardyment concludes that 'Mrs Gaskell and her daughter Marianne, rather than sad Samuel Butler, should be taken as the norm for the [Victorian] period' (Hardyment, p. 63).

In addition to its historical value, Mrs Gaskell's diary is significant as her first sustained piece of writing. '[A] good writer of fiction must have *lived* an active and sympathetic life', Gaskell advised an aspiring female author, and her own diary is a testament to such a life with her children (*Letters*, no. 515, p. 695). Without sentimentality or condescension, Gaskell chronicled the pleasures and dilemmas of daily life with a keen sense of observation, sympathy, curiosity, and humour – the qualities which would later characterize her fiction.

As a recent study has observed, Elizabeth Gaskell possessed an exceptional 'receptivity to the detail of daily life' and emphasized the importance of specific details in fiction (Stoneman, p. 37). '[Y]ou have to recollect & describe & report fully & accurately', Gaskell admonished a would-be novelist, and she followed her own advice (*Letters*, no. 420, p. 542). Concrete details were essential not only to create lively and engaging narratives, but to enhance readers' understanding of issues raised by such provocative novels as *Mary Barton*, *North and South*, and *Ruth*. Furthermore, Gaskell saw connections between a female perspective and the ability to provide and to appreciate seemingly small details. Hungry for information about a friend's wedding, she humorously exhorted the bride's father: '[O]h! do be a woman, and give me all possible details ...' (*Letters*, no. 419, p. 540). Likewise, she wanted a full report from Marianne's future husband about his trip to America and wryly requested 'little details which it is "beneath the dignity of man" to put on paper ...' (*Letters*, no. 409, p. 524). Gaskell was laughing at herself – one of her most appealing qualities – but she was also taking a friendly dig at the ineptitude of her male correspondents. Seeing the little things was a feminine gift too easily disparaged by men.

Gaskell's belief that life is in the details resembles Sara Ruddick's theory of 'maternal thinking', as described by Stoneman: 'the linking of knowledge with care, and the rooting of both in tiny, changing details' (Stoneman, p. 182). According to Ruddick's theory, mothers develop this special form of attentiveness in caring for children day by day; it is a moral and intellectual quality which derives from, and encourages, nurturance rather than dominance (Stoneman, p. 37). Gaskell's diary is an excellent example of 'maternal thinking' at work. Moreover, it suggests that the sympathetic insight characteristic of her novels was stimulated by her reflections upon the details of daily life with a young child. Gaskell's objective was not merely to record vignettes but to understand Marianne better by writing about her; noticing 'what' happened moved Gaskell to consider 'why'. For instance, Gaskell worried that Marianne was overly sensitive; she wept if she couldn't understand a joke and had a laugh which quickly turned to tears. Having observed these situations closely, Gaskell did not criticize Marianne but concluded that a lack of sympathy with the child's 'serious & thoughtful feelings' made her cry (p. 56). When Marianne was reluctant to join her parents at morning prayers, Gaskell attributed her behaviour to 'nervous shyness' and considered whether the religious service might be too long for a small child (p. 70). Perhaps Gaskell remembered Marianne's easily misunderstood sensitivity when she created the character of young Molly Gibson in *Wives and Daughters*, who suffers from teasing by a jocular adult and dreads bidding her hostess a formal farewell at a house party: 'All that blank space had to be crossed; and then a speech to be made!'

In one of the diary's more painful episodes, Marianne momentarily rejected her mother in favour of her nurse: '... MA absolutely pushed me away, fearing I should take her', Gaskell reported with some chagrin. In recording this incident, however, she sought to understand what had happened from her child's point of view. Marianne's nurse, 'having more bodily strength can amuse her more than I can ...', Gaskell concluded, and she resolved not to manipulate her daughter's affections (p. 56).

The process of recording and contemplating her maternal observations apparently helped Gaskell to accept, indeed to enjoy, her children's quite different personalities after the birth of her second daughter, Meta, in February 1837. 'I have been amused on looking at my former writing in this book to perceive the difference between the two little girls', she wrote when Meta was fourteen months and Marianne three and a half years old (p. 68). Her pithy and insightful character sketches depicted the quirks of temperament which revealed each child's individuality. At the age of four, Marianne was sensitive and sympathetic, although lacking in perseverance and liable to fits of obstinacy. Gaskell remarked upon her older daughter's concern for the poor and noted affectionately that Marianne 'tries so to comfort me if she sees me looking sad ...' (p. 70). At Meta's age, Marianne had presented a rather wistful picture; Gaskell described her 'sitting on the floor [when] a plaything rolls away, she has no idea of scrambling after it, but looks up beseechingly for someone to help her' (p. 58). Meta, 'totally different' from her sister, was more lively and outgoing, a 'little, saucy girl', as Gaskell humorously described her (pp. 70, 66). Less sensitive than Marianne, Meta enjoyed jokes and cared not at all if someone laughed at her. She was also 'very full of caprices' and sometimes 'passionate and wilful' (pp. 69, 70). Gaskell predicted that Meta would be 'more clever than her elder sister, if not so gentle' (p. 66).

Having two children to nurture and write about gave Gaskell a sense of perspective and greater scope for the analysis of character. She was intrigued not only by the differences in her daughters' behaviour but by possible reasons for their contrasting personalities. Remarking upon Meta's energy and confidence, Gaskell reminded herself that Meta had enjoyed more robust health than Marianne. She also speculated that Marianne, sensitive and vulnerable, had been affected by the death of Gaskell's beloved Aunt Lumb while Marianne was visiting her. Occasional conflicts between the children led Gaskell to conclude that a desire for power, rather than a lack of love, explained Marianne's domineering behaviour toward her younger sister. On a small scale, Gaskell was beginning to explore motives and personalities through writing and to lay a foundation for her future career.

Balancing the roles of wife, mother and writer was a perpetual challenge for Gaskell – by turns exhausting and exhilarating. Her letters provide an enlightening context for appreciating her diary as woman's 'herstory' as well as social history, while the diary in turn illuminates the letters. Writing to Eliza ('Tottie') Fox, a close friend and professional artist whose father sponsored the Married Women's Property Act, Gaskell summed up a dilemma in 1850 which remains all too familiar to women today:

> [A]ssuredly a blending of the two is desirable. (Home duties and the development of the Individual I mean), which you will say it takes no Solomon to tell you but the difficulty is where and when to make one set of duties subserve and give place to the other. I have no doubt that the cultivation of each tends to keep the other in a healthy state ... (*Letters*, no. 68, p. 106)

Some of Gaskell's early letters, written concurrently with her diary, reveal that she experienced this conflict of roles quite acutely during her first years of parenthood. An entry in the diary described motherhood as the culmination of a woman's existence, 'the period when she will be fulfilling one of her greatest & highest duties ...' (p. 53). This statement is more than a reiteration of a Victorian cliché; Gaskell perceived motherhood as one dimension, not the only function, of a woman's life. On the whole, however, the diary affirms the worth and importance of motherhood. Perhaps it would have been disturbing to discuss feelings of regret or restriction in the pages devoted to Marianne and intended for her future reading. Gaskell's 'implied reader' was Marianne as an adult, who would gain access through her mother's diary to the formative years which were crucial to her development but beyond reach of her own memory. In recording these memories, Gaskell assumed the opportunity and risk of shaping Marianne's future attitude toward herself and toward the idea of motherhood. It is therefore understandable that Gaskell was more inclined to voice ambivalence in letters to a network of sympathetic correspondents. A receptive audience could validate her emotions and mitigate a sense of isolation when parental obligations became oppressive.

In 1836, the Gaskells undertook a joint project of essays in verse, composed in the style of various poets. During a country visit to her mother's family home at Sandlebridge, Mrs Gaskell worked in an idyllic setting, which she described to her sister-in-law in a letter overflowing with happy details: 'the song of birds, the hum of insects the lowing of cattle' and Marianne 'at the very tip-top of bliss …' (*Letters*, no. 4, pp. 5–6). As Gaskell observed, this was an ideal environment for studying Romantic poetry. Nevertheless, she felt painfully isolated as a writer: 'If you were here, I think your advice, & listening, would do me so much good – but I have to do it all by myself alone, crunching up my paper, & scuttering my pencil away, when any one comes near' (*Letters*, no. 4, p. 7). Writer's frustration did not spoil Gaskell's delight in the bucolic surroundings and in Marianne's pleasure, but one form of satisfaction could not compensate for another. The anger and impatience which she repeatedly deplored in her diary may have stemmed from the tensions expressed in letters.

Two years later, in a letter to William and Mary Howitt, Gaskell again turned to rural imagery to express unfulfilled longings in an existence bound by the city of Manchester and the demands of two small daughters. Like a bird awakened by the stirrings of spring, Gaskell wrote, she longed to escape. More a realist than a romantic, she brought herself down to earth with a combination of humour and resignation: 'But as I happen to be a woman instead of a bird, as I have ties at home and duties to perform, and as, moreover … if I travel I must go by coach, and "remember the coachman," why I must stay at home and content myself with recalling the happy scenes which your books bring up before me' (*Letters*, no. 8, p. 14).

As the Gaskell family expanded, life as mother and writer became more complicated. In a rare interval of tranquillity ('Willie asleep everyone else out') on a Sunday morning in the summer of 1845, Gaskell furnished her sister-in-law, Eliza (Lizzy) Holland, with a mock-serious account of daily life:

I have Florence & Willie in my room which is also nursery, call Hearn at six, ½ p. 6 she is dressed, comes in, dresses Flora, gives her breakfast the first; ½ p. 7 I get up, 8 Flora goes down to her sisters & Daddy, & Hearn to her breakfast. While I in my dressing gown dress Willie. ½ p. 8 I go to breakfast with parlour people, Florence being with us & Willie (ought to be) in his cot; Hearn makes beds etc in nursery only. 9 she takes F. & I read chapter & have prayers first with household & then with children, ½ p. 9 Florence & Willie come in drawing room for an hour while bedroom & nursery windows are open; ½ p. 10 go in kitchen, cellars & order dinner. Write letters; ¼ p. 11 put on things; ½ p. 11 take Florence out. I come in, nurse W. & get ready for dinner; ½ p. 1 dinner; ½ p. 2 children, two little ones, come down during servants' dinner half hour open windows upstairs; 3 p.m. go up again & I have two hours to kick my heels in (to be elegant & explicit). 5 Marianne & Meta from lessons & Florence from upstairs & Papa when he can comes in drawing room to 'Lilly a hornpipe', i.e. dance while Mama plays, & make all the noise they can. Daddy reads, writes or does what she [he?] likes in dining room. ½ p. 5 Margaret (nursemaid) brings Florence's supper, which Marianne gives her, being answerable for slops, dirty pinafores & untidy misbehaviours while Meta goes up stairs to get ready & fold up Willie's basket of clothes while he is undressed (this by way of feminine & family duties). Meta is so neat & so knowing, only, handles wet napkins very gingerly. 6 I carry Florence up-stairs, nurse Willie; while she is tubbed & put to bed. ½ past 6 I come down dressed leaving (hitherto) both asleep & Will & Meta dressed (between 6 and ½ p.) & Miss F. with tea quite ready. [28] After tea read to M.A. & Meta till bedtime while they sew, knit or worsted work. From 8 till 10 gape. We are so desperately punctual that now you may know what we are doing every hour. (*Letters*, no. 16a, pp. 823–4)

Gaskell's portrait of Victorian domestic bliss resembles a film on fast forward and reveals the unromantic nuts and bolts of organization which enabled the family to function. She both exemplifies and satirizes the cultural imperative of household management, with the wife, as Mrs Beeton would say, like 'the commander of an army' (Beeton, p. 1). In spelling out every detail of daily routine, Gaskell demonstrates that even small tasks were planned and assigned not only to get everything done, but to teach the older girls responsibility. Her sense of humour enabled Gaskell to regard this beehive of purposeful activity with a degree of wry detachment. Moreover, she used her housewifely managerial skills to carve out some private time, which she described in terms defiant of mandates against female self-fulfilment and self-indulgence. Gaskell carried out admirably Mrs Ellis's exhortation to turn health, time and resources to the best account, but she did not hesitate to consider 'what shall I do to gratify myself ... or to vary the tenor of my existence?', questions which Mrs Ellis warned that 'a woman of right feelings' did not entertain. She was assured of a sympathetic audience for her letter. Lizzy Holland had several children at the time, would eventually have ten altogether, and herself worked at writing and translating.

Numerous letters through the years juxtapose literary discourse with domestic details in a vivid rush of catch-as-catch-can writing. 'I am ashamed of this letter'; Gaskell wrote in 1850, 'but unless I write in a hurry I never seem to find time to write at all' (*Letters*, no. 86, pp. 139–40). Ten years later, Gaskell still found it 'difficult to get even an uninterrupted 5 minutes, now we have all four daughters at home; for I like to keep myself in readiness to give them sympathy or advice at any moment ...' (*Letters*, no. 480, p. 640). 'If I had a library like yours, all undisturbed for hours, how I would write!' she declared enviously in a letter to her American friend and correspondent, Charles Eliot Norton (*Letters*, no. 384, p. 489). One of Gaskell's more poignant accounts of the sacrifices that she sometimes had to make appeared in a letter to Eliza Fox in 1852, when Gaskell 'was writing away vigorously at Ruth ...'. Company arrived, and she was obliged to play the hostess: '... I was sorry, *very* sorry to give it up my heart being so full of it, in a way which I can't bring back. That's *that*' (*Letters*, no. 137, p. 205). The emphatic conclusion implies both regret and a firm refusal to indulge in self-pity.[29]

When Gaskell did have 'a room of one's own', the seclusion felt strange. One senses that she not only survived, but thrived in a hectic family atmosphere which affirmed connectedness rather than isolation. 'I am so queer and desolate today', she confided to Catherine Winkworth, 'everybody being gone, and I not yet understanding solitude and husbandless independence!' (*Letters*, no. 35, p. 66). Occasional respites from family demands were welcome; in another letter, Gaskell revelled in her temporary freedom as a 'gypsy-bachelor', with no one's needs except her own to consider (*Letters*, no. 206, p. 301).[30] But it is hard to imagine her happily inhabiting Norton's ivory tower for any length of time. After envying his library, she regaled him with a memorable catalogue of everyday duties; her tone suggests a spirit of zest and humour rather than domestic drudgery:

> Now in this hour since breakfast I have had to decide on the following variety of important questions. Boiled beef – how long to boil? What perennials will do in Manchester smoke, & what colours our garden wants? Length of skirt for a gown? Salary of a nursery governess, & stipulations for a certain quantity of time to be left to herself [perhaps the employer envied the employee this luxury]. – Read letters on the state of Indian army – lent me by a very agreeable neighbour & return them, with a proper note, & as many wise remarks as would come in a hurry. Settle 20 questions of dress for the girls, who are going out for the day; & want to look nice & yet not spoil their gowns with the mud &c &c – See a lady about an MS story of hers, & give her disheartening but very good advice. Arrange about selling two poor cows for one good one, – see purchasers, & show myself up to cattle questions, keep, & prices, – and it's not ½ past 10 yet! (*Letters*, no. 384, pp. 489–90)

Amid a whirlwind of household accomplishments, Gaskell's role as a writer receives no more nor less attention than her other activities; it is part of an ordinary day. Her letter might have served as an exemplum in Isabella Beeton's *Book of Household Management*, but Mrs Beeton would not have approved of a wife and mother pursuing a career other than her family. Ironically, Gaskell's effective and energetic management of household, children, finances, and social obligations made her an excellent Victorian housewife while simultaneously undermining conventional domesticity.

Gaskell's letter to Norton brings her literary and maternal vocations full circle. In telling him about the publication of a short story, 'The Doom of the Griffiths' (and her shrewd efforts to ensure payment from the publisher), she also revealed that she had begun the story more than twenty years earlier, when Marianne was a baby. As Jenny Uglow has pointed out in her recent biography, Gaskell never stopped writing, even when her children were young; her 'nurture of real and fictitious people was inextricably linked' (Uglow, p. 128).[31] Although the diary makes no reference to any such literary endeavours, it does occasionally hint that Gaskell worried about not devoting herself sufficiently to her children. When Marianne began infant school, Gaskell wondered uneasily if she were abdicating some of her maternal responsibility, 'becoming a lazy mother, willing to send my children away from me ...' (p. 67).

The diary was a legitimate retreat, a private legacy for Marianne which also offered an opportunity for respite and self-expression. Writing for publication, on the other hand, raised thorny issues of egoism and responsibility. 'If Self is to be the end of exertions, those exertions are unholy, there is no doubt of *that* ...', Gaskell asserted in 1850. She proceeded to grapple with the complexity of selfhood and ambition: '... first we must find out what we are sent into the world to do, and define it and make it clear to ourselves, (that's *the* hard part) and then forget ourselves in our work ...' (*Letters*, no. 68, p. 107).

A family tragedy became the impetus for Gaskell's career as a novelist. After her infant son's death in 1845, she desperately needed to 'forget herself in her work' and began writing *Mary Barton* with the moral support of her husband. The novel was published anonymously in 1848.[32] In her preface to the first edition, Gaskell made an oblique reference to the personal loss which had moved her to undertake her first book: 'Three years ago I became anxious (from circumstances that need not be more fully alluded to) to employ myself in writing a work of fiction.' However, her first novel was much more than an eloquent sublimation of maternal grief. *Mary Barton* represents a fusion of personal loss and social consciousness with Gaskell's emergent self-definition as a writer. Her experience of motherhood, attachment, devotion, and bereavement permeated the novel's moral vision and invigorated Gaskell's criticism of the poverty which accompanied Manchester's industrial boom. Injustice strikes home when the worker John Barton confronts a well-intentioned representative of the city's more prosperous inhabitants: 'Ay, ma'am, but have ye ever seen a child clemmed [starved] to death?'[33]

Verisimilitude animated by sympathy earned praise from readers and reviewers of *Mary Barton*, who recognized the cumulative power of seemingly insignificant details to move an audience and ultimately to shake the social conscience of 'people on Turkey carpets, with their three meat meals-a-day, [who] are wondering, forsooth, why working men turn Chartists and Communists' (Charles Kingsley, qtd. in Easson, p. 153). More temperate than Kingsley's fulmination in *Fraser's Magazine*, John Forster's review in the *Examiner* looked more closely at the nuances of Gaskell's writing: 'shrewd perception' of character, whether rich or poor; a reservoir of 'quiet quaint humour'; insight into 'the motives which actuate ordinary life'; and knowledge of what Forster rather vaguely termed 'the higher and more out-of-the-way regions of existence' made for literary 'power of a rare and unquestionable kind...' (qtd. in Easson, p. 69). Noting 'the delicate points of the portraiture' of women and children and the 'minuteness of the domestic details', Forster concluded that a woman had written *Mary Barton* (qtd. in Easson, p. 68). As Angus Easson has pointed out, the association of such qualities with women's writing was not patronizing, as it might appear today, but rather a tribute to women's 'distinctive capacities of feeling and knowledge', especially the ability to create compelling and credible narratives through sharp perception and skillful selection of details (Easson, p. 2). At least one critic discerned the personal subtext of *Mary Barton*. Writing in the *Revue Européenne* in 1861, Charles de Moüy stated that no writer understood so well as Gaskell 'those griefs that survive the passage of time and know neither consolation nor oblivion' (qtd. in Easson, p. 501).

'I pray you to tell me who wrote *Mary Barton*', Maria Edgeworth cajoled Gaskell's cousin, Mary Holland. Like Forster, Edgeworth had surmised that the novelist was 'a *she*' whose 'power of drawing *from* the life and *to* the life' rested upon deft application of 'all those small details which can be obtained only from personal observation ...'. Richness of experience did not necessarily make a novelist, however, nor did Edgeworth accept emotional impact as a sufficient criterion for a female writer's success. '[O]nly by the union of quick feeling with cool discriminating judgment' could the essence of one's deeply felt experience be distilled and conveyed to readers.[34] Gaskell's diary, unbeknownst to Edgeworth, had provided this ideal combination of intense involvement and disciplined objectivity.

In cultivating her powers of observation, the initially small and private world of Gaskell's diary may have laid a foundation for the wider social vision articulated in her novels. In 1850, a letter to Dickens described Gaskell's efforts on behalf of an imprisoned teenage prostitute, who had committed robbery and contemplated suicide. A greater contrast with Gaskell's own daughters could scarcely be imagined. Yet beneath the delinquent's exterior, Gaskell saw a neglected child 'with a wild wistful look in her eyes, as if searching for the kindness she has never known ...' (*Letters*, no. 61, p. 99). The childlike vulnerability which elicited Gaskell's sympathy was enhanced by the girl's family history: '... her mother had shown most complete indifference to her', Gaskell wrote in outrage (*Letters*, no. 61, p. 98). Young Miss Pasley was a victim not only of the doctor who had seduced her, but of the mother who had ignored her daughter's desperate letters. It is possible, of course, that Gaskell was merely seeing what she wanted to see; an innocent girl gone wrong was more appealing than a hardened criminal. But evading harsh realities was not Gaskell's style, and the incident is representative of her ability to reach beyond the boundaries of appearance and social class to see the person within. Hilary Schor has suggested that this encounter inspired Gaskell to begin writing *Ruth* (Schor, p. 45). Gaskell's perceptive gifts, enhanced by her diary, were not limited to her own children.

Mrs Gaskell's diary ends shortly after Marianne's fourth birthday, in the autumn of 1838. There is no indication that Gaskell was deliberately concluding the diary at this point; presumably she became too busy to resume it, and it consequently fell by the wayside.[35] What became of Marianne and Meta as they grew up, and what impact did their early upbringing have upon their development? What were Gaskell's ideas about child-rearing as her children matured? Her letters give some answers. Gaskell's voluminous correspondence with Marianne provides a continuing chronicle of the mother–daughter relationship, as the delicate but stubborn little girl portrayed in the diary became a young woman and her mother's confidante. Ironically, the survival of these letters would not have pleased Gaskell, who wanted her private correspondence destroyed. Scholars may be thankful that Marianne, perhaps preserving a bit of her childhood obstinacy, disobeyed her mother's repeated injunction to 'burn any letters'.

The diary's images of Marianne as a small child continued to influence how Gaskell perceived her eldest daughter. Did Marianne's character develop with remarkable consistency from her earliest years, or had Gaskell's writing created a 'fixed text', which became a self-fulfilling prophecy as Marianne matured? Three years after her last diary entry, Gaskell wrote a heartfelt letter asking her sister-in-law, Anne Robson, to watch over Marianne. Pregnant and unwell, Gaskell felt vulnerable and feared that, like her own mother, she would not live to raise her children. 'It is difficult to have the right trust in God almost, when thinking about one's children' (*Letters*, no. 16, p. 46).[36] Her concern was not for their material well-being, but she worried that others – even her husband – were not equipped to look beneath the surface of a child's behaviour and understand the subtleties of character. Meta was 'remarkably independent', as she had been even as a toddler, but Marianne had an exceptional need for affection and sympathy: 'The want of them would make MA an unhappy character, probably sullen & deceitful – while the sunshine of love & tenderness would do everything for her' (*Letters*, no. 16, p. 46).

Gaskell was anxious not only that Marianne be loved but that her rather difficult temperament be understood. Over the years, Gaskell continued to struggle with Marianne's quirks of character, while enjoying a close and mutually supportive relationship with her eldest daughter. She was never too busy to write to her 'dearest Polly'.[37] 'My darling', Gaskell scribbled in one of her hurried but affectionate missives, 'if [this] only tells you a little bit how dearly I love you that will do for the present, won't it?' (*Letters*, no. 205, p. 300).

Gaskell's love for Marianne was unconditional but not indiscriminate. Like her diary, her letters to and about Marianne evince profound affection without doting sentimentality or evasion of painful realities. Gaskell was most appreciative when eighteen-year-old Marianne offered to serve as a temporary governess for Florence and Julia. She praised Marianne's '*moral management*' of the younger girls (*Letters*, no. 141, p. 212), worried about taking advantage of her services, and admired her self-discipline and 'grave steady resolution' (*Letters*, no. 146, p. 219). The problem child had become a pillar of strength. But along with maternal pride and gratitude, Gaskell's letters sounded a recurrent note of regret that Marianne was all too happy to settle for less than her full potential – an issue which had perplexed Gaskell since Marianne's childhood. '[S]he never reads', Gaskell lamented, 'but generally does the practical and polite and elder daughter things in the house' (*Letters*, no. 421, p. 544). This was a typical Victorian role for an as yet unmarried adult daughter, but Gaskell valued aspiration over complacent contentment. 'Remember', she cautioned Marianne, 'your error always is repeating people's *praises* of you, and *omitting*, (I really think you *forget*) their blame or fault-finding' (*Letters*, no. 116, p. 179).

When Marianne ventured beyond the domestic sphere, the results could be disconcerting. At age sixteen, she adopted an anti-protectionist stance which clashed with her family's politics. Her parents were not impressed by her inability to provide reasoned arguments for her position. Suspecting that Marianne was easily captivated by outside influences, William and Elizabeth demanded an account of her political opinions, 'straight from yourself without your asking any one' (*Letters*, no. 91b, p. 834). Furthermore, Mrs Gaskell did not want her daughter to reinforce the prevalent stereotype of ill-informed women meddling in politics; instead, she recommended that the decidedly unintellectual Marianne join her in reading William Cobden and Adam Smith.

In politics or religion, 'you must have a "reason for the faith that is in you"', Gaskell advised (*Letters*, no. 93, p. 148). She and Marianne both enjoyed attending Anglican services, but Mrs Gaskell warned Miss Gaskell not to 'offend one's sense of *truth*' by indulging in such practices too frequently. Aesthetic pleasure in church-going was not spirituality, nor was religion a refuge from the demands of rigorous thought. Reflecting on her own behalf as well as Marianne's, Gaskell concluded that 'we can not love [God and Christ] properly unless we try and define them clearly to ourselves' (*Letters*, no. 198a, p. 860).

Some years later, Marianne created a family melodrama when she acquired a temporary fascination with Catholicism. The allurement of Anglican church services paled in comparison to the threat of Papism in the Gaskell household. In 1857, Elizabeth, Marianne, and Meta had made their first visit to Rome. This was one of the happiest episodes in Mrs Gaskell's life, and the beginning of her enduring friendship with Charles Eliot Norton.[38] The Unitarian visitors received intense and not altogether welcome attention from Henry Manning, the future Cardinal, and from other converts who hoped to win them over. Marianne returned to Rome with friends during the winter of 1861–2. On this occasion, her encounters with Manning made a deeper impression, to the consternation of her parents. Mrs Gaskell reacted as if Marianne were an impressionable teenager instead of a twenty-seven-year-old woman. '… but oh! if I do but hear good accounts of you my child … that you are pretty strong, that you are not led off by excitement to go a few steps (as you think *only*) on a wrong & terrible way …' (*Letters*, no. 500a, p. 921).

As Uglow has observed, Gaskell was reluctant to relinquish control over her adult children. If flirting with Catholicism was Marianne's idea of widening her horizons, perhaps she should leave theology and politics to her parents. A course of reading with her father was prescribed to counteract the 'evil influence' of Romanism, but Marianne lacked the aptitude and inclination to formulate her own beliefs with the intellectual rigour which her parents valued: '*Arguments* never did seem to have much force for her in *abstract* things', Gaskell observed with resignation. 'She is one of the clearest people I know about *practical* things … Set against that *great* unselfishness & sweetness, & meekness' (*Letters*, no. 504, p. 683).

Meta was quite a different story, as might be expected from glimpses of her early character in Gaskell's diary. Unlike Marianne, Meta shared her mother's intellectual and artistic interests and was precocious to boot. Gaskell reported that, at fourteen, Meta was '*quite* able to appreciate any book I am reading' (*Letters*, no. 101, p. 161). Meta had fulfilled her mother's prophecy that she would be more clever than Marianne; again, the consistency of character begs the question of whether the diary's predictions became self-perpetuating. But however gratified Gaskell may have been to discover a soul-mate in her second daughter, she did not idealize Meta's artistic temperament. If Marianne was a bit too practical-minded, Meta was 'untidy, dreamy, and absent' (*Letters*, no. 101, p. 161) and had 'almost too many interests' (*Letters*, no. 421, p. 544) which interfered with routine duties. Gaskell cherished both daughters, and her letters reveal the same respect for each girl's individuality as did the diary many years before. Having grown up with only occasional contact with her much older brother, Gaskell especially appreciated the closeness between her elder daughters, despite their differences in personality. 'Minnie's contrast of character works so admirably on Meta; – and the Sisters are so fond of each other', she remarked with pleasure when both girls had grown into womanhood (*Letters*, no. 553, p. 736).

Meta, whom Gaskell had once counted on to strengthen Marianne, became more vulnerable in her early adulthood and needed the tonic of Marianne's 'good sense & merry ways' (*Letters*, no. 394, p. 506). In 1857, at the age of twenty, Meta had suddenly fallen in love with Captain Charles Hill, an army officer from India and a widower some years her senior. Her parents were less than enthusiastic about this impulsive romance, but they treated Meta's fiancé cordially. They were equally supportive when Meta decided to end the engagement, after she discovered that Captain Hill had not been honest with her regarding his finances and business dealings. 'I am sure she has done right', Mrs Gaskell wrote to Charles Norton. Meta was 'far from well', but Gaskell attributed her daughter's troubles to 'deep disappointment in character' rather than 'wounded affection' (Letters, no. 394, p. 506). Possibly Gaskell was reluctant to admit that Meta may indeed have been in love with a man of whom her parents disapproved. '[I] don't think she ever thinks of her year of engagement', Gaskell wrote in a letter to Eliza Fox a year later (Letters, no. 421, p. 544).

However, Meta suffered from persistent health problems which, as Gaskell acknowledged, were probably psychosomatic. '[S]he has a horror of being thought hysterical but I think these fits of crying are of that nature …', Gaskell wrote to Anne Robson early in 1865 (Letters, no. 558, p. 741). A severe winter three years previously had exacerbated Meta's symptoms. When Manchester's textile mills were cut off from their cotton supplies during the American Civil War, massive unemployment followed with all of its attendant hardships. The Gaskell women worked ten-hour days in charity relief. Marianne's practical competence enabled her to cope without too much angst; the little girl who 'would give rather too freely to the poor' (p. 68) had acquired her mother's compassionate yet unsentimental attitude. But Meta agonized over the suffering she witnessed, 'laboured day and night in weighing and planning and thinking', and consequently fell ill from stress (Letters, no. 526, p. 707). The advice of 'a great famous London surgeon' (Letters, no. 560, p. 744) anticipated the oppressive rest cure described in Charlotte Perkins Gilman's short story, 'The Yellow Wall-Paper'. Meta was 'not to read deep books,' to visit the poor, or to do anything else which might cause her anxiety. She was placed under a psychological quarantine which constrained normal family life, at least in the bustling and intellectually stimulating Gaskell household. 'So she, to whom we all went for sympathy and advice leads a life as apart from ours as we can make it … we have continually to check ourselves to keep her in peace' (Letters, no. 560, p. 745).

Gaskell's account contrasts sadly with earlier descriptions of Meta as a robust, saucy little girl and as an energetic young woman who danced all evening and had a prodigious appetite for dinners and books. Although she did not spend the rest of her life as a wounded romantic, Meta remained single and never fully recovered her strength. After the engagement fiasco, Gaskell believed that Meta was entitled to a life of her own as a professional artist. Despite personal talent and parental encouragement, an artistic career presented manifold challenges in an age which lauded woman as 'the angel in the house'. Mrs Gaskell's own formidable success may also have been intimidating to an emotionally fragile daughter. Meta created her own niche as a single woman with a variety of interests – art, music, politics, and mountain-climbing on Alpine holidays. She and her youngest sister, Julia, kept house for their father after Mrs Gaskell's sudden death in 1865, but they were hardly conventional spinsters. Active in Manchester social work, they enjoyed frequent travels and a lively circle of friends, quite a contrast to Charlotte Brontë's image of 'sour old maids, anxious, backbiting, wretched, because life is a desert to them' (*Shirley*, ch. 22). Meta continued to need emotional support, however, and her own health declined after Julia's death in 1908. Meta died five years later.

Having two unmarried daughters was not a disappointment to Mrs Gaskell. She respected single women and had portrayed a vital and supportive community of women in *Cranford*. Her comments on marriage and single life do suggest that she felt a lack of 'natural duties as wives & mothers' in the lives of unmarried women, who 'must look out for other duties if they wish to be at peace' (*Letters*, no. 72, p. 117). Like Florence Nightingale, another of her numerous correspondents, Gaskell abhorred the image of purposeless women with 'Nothing to Do' – the title of one of Nightingale's essays.[39] No doubt she would have been gratified by Meta's and Julia's mutual companionship and social activism.

Marriage presented its own set of challenges and hazards, not the least of which was finding suitable husbands. Mrs Gaskell lamented the dearth of young Unitarian men who possessed the intellectual and spiritual qualities 'which those *must* appreciate who would think of my girls' (*Letters*, no. 453, p. 598). Florence's husband, Charles Crompton, did not quite make the grade at first. Gaskell credited him with good character, but in her shrewd assessment he lacked 'imagination enough to be what one calls *spiritual*' (*Letters*, no. 526, p. 706). It was hard for Mrs Gaskell to see 'Flossy' as a young woman rather than a child, and she was not ready to surrender her influence over her third daughter. '[S]he is very young for her age,' Gaskell pontificated, '& as yet requires the daily elevation of her thoughts & aims' (*Letters*, no. 546, p. 725).

Like Marianne, Florence had proved to be rather disappointing in matters of the intellect, preferring 'little housewife things to anything presenting the least intellectual *effort* …' (*Letters*, no. 476, p. 632). Gaskell hoped, in a somewhat pompous vein, that marriage would lead Florence 'into the standard of high goodness of which she [was] thoroughly capable' (*Letters*, no. 546, p. 725). Apparently it did not; a year after her wedding, 'Dear little Florence [was] curiously unchanged by marriage …' But the union was a happy one, and Mrs Gaskell warmed to her son-in-law's steady and unpretentious character. In fact, she worried that Florence was 'a little bit tyrannical over her sweet-tempered husband in her own house' (*Letters*, no. 551, p. 733).

Florence had surprised her family by becoming engaged at twenty. Marianne, on the other hand, married her second cousin, Thurstan Holland, whom she had known since childhood – rather like marrying the proverbial boy next door, except that Marianne's eight-year romance stirred up a family tempest. 'He is *very* good, very intelligent, very gentlemanly, & very full of fun; aged 22, Eton & Trin. Coll. Cam.' (*Letters*, no. 388, p. 498). Elizabeth Gaskell penned this brief but enthusiastic character sketch of Thurstan Holland in April 1858, shortly before he began a trip to America. Bright but not solemn, fun but not shallow, Thurstan possessed just the qualities which Gaskell not only approved, but delighted in. She warmly recommended him to her American acquaintances and shamelessly pumped him for information when he returned to England.'Oh! you *must* come & be gossipy in Plymouth Grove', Gaskell cajoled with easy familiarity (*Letters*, no. 409, p. 524). Two months later, Thurstan was studying law in London while maintaining 'a brisk correspondence with Marianne ...' (*Letters*, no. 418, p. 538). When Cambridge lost to Oxford in the annual boat-race that summer of 1859, Marianne received some good-natured teasing from her family, who did not take her fondness for Thurstan very seriously.

By the spring of 1860, however, something had occurred which made Gaskell 'silently & quietly much displeased' with Thurstan (*Letters*, no. 461, p. 610).[40] His father, Edward Holland, strongly disapproved of the relationship between Thurstan and Marianne. As the oldest son in a very large family, Thurstan was expected to '"marry money"', as Gaskell bluntly reminded Marianne in a letter which cited Charles Darwin's sister Catherine as a possible candidate whom 'Dumbleton would not dislike ...' (*Letters*, no. 484b, p. 919) – Dumbleton Hall was the Holland's Gloucestershire country estate. Gaskell may have feared that Marianne would be hurt if Thurstan continued his attentions against his father's will, or she may have been disappointed in Thurstan for allegedly 'making up to Miss Darwin ...' (*Letters*, no. 484b, p. 919). After Meta's traumatic experience with Captain Hill, it would have been natural for Gaskell to protect Marianne (and herself, perhaps) from another such painful episode. But this is one secret which Gaskell kept, and the particular reason for her change of heart toward Thurstan has never come to light.

In the summer of 1862, Marianne spent some time at Dumbleton after returning from her brush with Catholicism in Rome. Then she met her mother, Meta and Florence in London. Thurstan's brother Fred was also in the city and bent over backwards to be helpful. His efforts were warmly received by Mrs Gaskell, who was ready to let bygones be bygones: '... he came every morng [sic] to help us & arrange plans during our stay, & was evidently most anxious to heal the old Thurstan breach ...', she wrote to Catherine Winkworth (*Letters*, no. 509b, pp. 927–8).

Thurstan invited the Gaskell party to Eton for the annual boat races and fireworks. The 'old row', as Gaskell called it, whatever it had been, was past history. The fireworks fizzled in a downpour of rain, but the races were a splendid spectacle:

Then they came with shout & song & music down the dark river ... out of the darkness into the shining water, – into the darkness again, – all the crews standing up motionless as they passed the brilliant illuminated 'Floreat Etona'. The thing reminded *me* of the Saxon Kings [*sic*] comparison of human life to the swallows flying thro' the tent, out of darkness coming, – into darkness going ... (*Letters*, no. 511a, p. 929)

Gaskell's poeticism ran out at the end of her letter, which concluded with the dismal fragment, 'Drenched & miserable.' For Marianne and Thurstan, the rainy day at Eton marked the beginning of their unofficial engagement. When the truth came out about two years later, the Gaskells accepted the situation, but Edward Holland was still adamantly opposed and behaved like a caricature of an autocratic Victorian father. He forbade not only Marianne, but Mrs Gaskell, to answer Thurstan's letters, and threatened to cut Thurstan off financially if he married Marianne. The 'pretty little family "tiff"' which resulted (*Letters*, no. 553, p. 737) weighed more heavily on Elizabeth and William than upon the young lovers, who were no longer quite so youthful when they finally married but had certainly 'been very constant to each other ...' (*Letters*, no. 560, p. 744). 'It has been a good deal of a worry; which we, not being in love, have felt a good deal more than the parties concerned' (*Letters*, no. 553, p. 736), Mrs Gaskell wrote, with the blend of humour and resignation which characterized many of her letters. This was the second time she had had to support a daughter through a problematic romance. It was not easy to relinquish her 'dearest Polly' to marriage, but Marianne's happiness prevailed over all obstacles: '... we don't mind a long engagement for we shall keep our child that much the longer', Gaskell confided to Charles Norton in February 1865 (*Letters*, no. 560, p. 744). A month earlier, Gaskell had assured her sister-in-law Anne Robson that Marianne was 'looking very well and very handsome; and altogether as young as her intended 18 months younger Thurstan' (*Letters*, no. 558, p. 741). The humorous reference to Marianne's age was probably a dig at Thurstan's father, who bolstered his financial argument against the marriage by ostensibly objecting to his son's union with a slightly older cousin.

Sadly, Mrs Gaskell did not live to see Marianne and Thurstan married. Their wedding took place on 14 August 1866, nine months after Gaskell's sudden death at the age of 55. One of her last letters was written to Thurstan in October 1865; an informal invitation, its unpretentious warmth shows that he was not only accepted, but embraced as part of the family:[41] 'Please we are quite hoping to see you on the 28th at "*The Lawn*" – you won't mind everything being rough. We can give you bread & cheese & cold meat, and "Alton Ale" & tea & bread & butter & "excellent milk" (Hearn says,) & a hearty welcome' (*Letters*, no. 587, pp. 779–80).[42] Thurstan, in his turn, paid tribute to Mrs Gaskell when he wrote to Charles Norton about her sudden death. Although Thurstan's sentiments were expressed in terms more conventional than original, they have the ring of genuine affection: '[...] I feel her loss very deeply for all who knew her well must have loved that kind sympathetic heart which shared every one's joys or griefs, that fresh intellect, that powerful imagination, that kindly interest that she took in every one about her' (18 November 1865; *Letters*, p. 971). And Gaskell would surely have appreciated Thurstan's conclusion, '[...] I have been obliged to write hurriedly [...]' (*Letters*, p. 971).[43]

Marianne and Thurstan had three children, who were the only direct descendants of William and Elizabeth Gaskell. Florence, who had no children, died in 1881. Marianne, sensible as ever, outlived her three younger sisters and enjoyed a vital life well into old age. Three years after her death in 1920, her mother's diary was printed in a limited edition. The original manuscript remained within the family until 1994, when it was deposited in the Brotherton Library of the University of Leeds.

Of all Gaskell's letters, one stands out as an apt summation of her diary's value, both as a personal document and as a precursor of her novels. In 1851, she provided Anne Robson with affectionate and discerning character sketches of the Gaskell daughters. Marianne, no scholar, had acquired self-discipline at boarding school and was already a 'patient steady' teacher of the two youngest girls during vacations. Except for her '*really* fine' singing, her accomplishments were unspectacular but solid. Meta, gifted but absent-minded, was 'a great darling in another way.' Not much use around the house, she was 'brim-full of I don't know what to call it, for it is something deeper, & less showy than talent.' Florence was a 'very nervous' nine-year-old, but Gaskell appreciated that much of her anxiety was 'on *other* people's behalf, not her own', which put Flossy's character in quite a different light. Perhaps coping with Marianne's early sensitivity had helped Gaskell to look beyond the surface of her third daughter's behaviour. Once equally vulnerable, Marianne now served as a 'capital confidante' for her younger sister. And Julia, the irrepressible baby of the family, was 'witty, & wild, & clever and droll ...' (*Letters*, no. 101, pp. 160–1).

'These are my 4 children', Gaskell concluded, 'for you must go on knowing them as they are, not their mere outsides ...' In similar words, Winifred Gérin has observed that Gaskell's 'unique achievement, both as a woman and an author', was getting to know the people she wrote about, 'from without and within, by the sheer sincerity of her sympathy and receptivity' (Gérin, p. 78). Gaskell's diary reveals the importance of her maternal role in developing these qualities. In addition to its value as a perceptive portrait of Victorian family life, Gaskell's chronicle of her early years of parenthood offers a unique perspective upon her 'distinctively humane ... combination of scrupulous observation and compassionate imagination' (Gilbert and Gubar, p. 311).

Notes

Page references are to the works listed in 'Works Cited'. References to Gaskell's letters are normally to J. A. V. Chapple and Arthur Pollard (eds), *The Letters of Mrs Gaskell* (Manchester UP, Manchester: 1966; American issue, Harvard UP, Cambridge, MA: 1967), cited as *Letters*. References to letters not published by Chapple and Pollard are given in full.

1. Marianne was the Gaskells' first surviving child; their first daughter was still-born in July 1833. This early bereavement was recalled in an unpublished sonnet by Mrs Gaskell, 'On Visiting the Grave of my Stillborn Little Girl', dated 4 July 1836 (printed in A. W. Ward's Biographical Introduction to Knutsford, I, xxvi–xxvii; qtd. in Uglow, pp. 91–2; see also Appendix IV below). The Gas-kells' three younger daughters, Margaret Emily ('Meta'), Florence Elizabeth, and Julia Bradford, were born in 1837, 1842, and 1846, respectively. Two sons died in infancy.

2. Page references to quotations from Gaskell's diary apply to this new edition; all punctuation and spelling have been reproduced.

3. Elizabeth Gaskell's first published work, *Sketches Among the Poor*, was an essay in verse written in collaboration with her husband and printed in *Blackwood's Edinburgh Magazine* in January 1837. It has been reprinted in the Biographical Introduction to Knutsford, I, xxii–xxiii, and as Appendix 2 in the Penguin Classics edition of *Mary Barton*, ed. Stephen Gill (1970).

4. On a happier note, Gaskell's father had encouraged her to write. William Stevenson was an early contributor to *Blackwood's Magazine* (where Elizabeth made her first appearance in print), and he sent his adolescent daughter copies and critiques of the *Literary Gazette*. '[I] expect you will keep a regular journal of what you see and remember', he informed Elizabeth in his one extant letter to her (2 July 1827; Chapple and Sharps, p. 5). Gaskell's only surviving sibling, John Stevenson, hoped to establish a writing career but was never published. Eleven years older than his sister, he recognized her potential. '[I]t would almost make the foundation of a novel –', he declared upon receiving one of Elizabeth's adolescent letters (30 July 1828; Chapple and Sharps, pp. 4–5).

5. The pervasive impact of Gaskell's loss is evident in her novels and stories; as Uglow has observed, most of her heroines are orphaned or motherless.

6. In his forthcoming book on Gaskell's early life, Chapple observes that 'it is truly extraordinary that [Gaskell] should have nothing whatsoever that had once been her mother's … that no keepsake had been left to her, no small object preserved by her father or sent down to Mrs Lumb for the little girl to have when she grew past babyhood.'

7. As Mrs Gaskell realized later, her husband's reluctance to discuss parental worries stemmed from his own propensity for anxiety, not from insensitivity. '[H]e is so *very* anxious when he *is* anxious', she wrote to Anne Robson, 'that I think he always dislikes being made to acknowledge there is cause' (*Letters*, no. 570, pp. 760–1).

8. In 1877, Bull's *Hints to Mothers* had reached its fourteenth edition; his *Maternal Management of Children in Health and Disease* (1840) had reached its eighth edition.

9.   *L'Education progressive* was published in two volumes, 1828–32, and was trans-
     lated into English in 1835. Gaskell read and quoted from the original French
     edition. *Progressive Education, with Notes, Appendix, and Translation by Emma
     Willard and Almira Phelps* (Boston: 1835) included Phelps's 'Observations on an
     Infant,' an account of her son's early life. Phelps followed de Saussure's advice
     to keep a maternal diary, and hers has much in common with Gaskell's in
     content and approach (Hardyment, p. 75).

10. Mrs Gaskell met Mme Mohl, who was popularly known as 'Clarkey', during a
     visit to Paris in 1853. Mohl held a salon graced by a cavalcade of illustrious
     acquaintances, including Robert and Elizabeth Barrett Browning, Harriet
     Martineau, George Eliot, William Thackeray, Victor Hugo, Ivan Turgenev, and
     Stendhal. She and Gaskell quickly became warm friends, and Mohl arranged
     for Louise Swanton, the wife of Hilaire Belloc, to translate *Cranford* into
     French. Uglow discusses Mohl's influence upon Gaskell's writing (Uglow,
     pp. 349–50). Mohl's correspondence includes her impression of Marianne
     Gaskell, then aged nineteen: '... Marianne is not that interesting with nothing
     of the beaming countenance of the mother. To my taste she is the most
     agreeable literary lady I have yet seen' (Mary Mohl to Elizabeth Reid, 17 [May
     1853], Reid Papers, qtd. in Uglow, p. 348).

11. *Sketch of the life, character and writings of the Baroness de Staël-Holstein* was
     published in an English translation in 1820. Mme de Staël had died in 1817.

12. Mme de Saussure had read some of Maria Edgeworth's books, as translated
     by Mme Swanton Belloc, and thought highly of Edgeworth.

13. Gaskell need not have worried. When Marianne was in her sixties, she warmly
     recalled a bond of intimacy and friendship which '... you do not often, I think,
     find between mother and daughter' (Marianne Gaskell Holland, qtd. by Lyall
     in Oliphant, p. 143). Marianne's public description of her mother as her 'great-
     est friend' resembles Gaskell's private account of her Aunt Lumb as her 'best
     friend' (p. 63). Whether or not Marianne deliberately echoed her mother's
     phrasing, the similarity represents what each woman perceived as most impor-
     tant about her actual or surrogate mother.

14. Gaskell may have been thinking of an aunt, whose upbringing she would later
     describe in chapter 3 of *The Life of Charlotte Brontë*. The girl was tossed in a
     blanket to strengthen her nerves. Such drastic measures were advocated by
     Thomas Day, a disciple of Rousseau who took the master's philosophy to
     extremes. *Émile* had reinforced Locke's advice, in *Some Thoughts Concerning
     Education* (1693), to impose physical discomforts upon children in order to
     strengthen their minds and bodies. Light clothing in cold weather, hard beds,
     and unpredictable mealtimes would make children sturdy and prevent them
     from becoming psychologically enslaved to creature comforts. This Spartan
     school of child development was clearly contrary to Combe's recommen-
     dation that any unnecessary irritations be avoided.

15. William Gaskell's brother Samuel (1807–86) was a physician and a leader in
     the movement against forcible restraint of mental patients. In 1840, he was
     elected Resident Surgeon at the Lancaster County Lunatic Asylum and imple-
     mented reforms which earned him the FRCS three years later. A prize in his
     name is awarded annually by the Royal College of Psychiatrists. Interestingly,
     he had paired forty orphans with forty female mental patients in order to

'develop in the women the great principle of maternal love' (qtd. in Elwood and Félicité, p. 90). 'Sam' Gaskell was Elizabeth's favorite brother-in-law, and her diary praises his care and concern for Marianne during an acute attack of croup. See also *Letters*, no. 7, p. 13, and Richard Hunter and Ida MacAlpine's introduction in John Conolly, *Treatment of the Insane Without Mechanical Restraints* (1856; Folkestone and London: 1973), pp. 295–6.

16.   Page numbers refer to the original sources as cited by Pollock, which include: Mary Sewell, *The Life and Letters of Mrs Sewell*, 3rd ed. (James Nisbet, London: 1889); *Memoirs and Letters of Sara Coleridge*, ed. by her daughter (Henry S. King and Co., London: 1873); Elizabeth Grant, *Memoirs of a Highland Lady*, ed. Lady Strachey (John Murray, London: 1911); E. Morgan (ed.), *Memoirs of the Late Mrs Mary Timms* (T. Whitehorn, London: 1835); Mary Elizabeth Haldane, *Record of a Hundred Years 1825–1925*, ed. by her daughter (Hodder and Stoughton, London: 1925).

17.   See note 16.

18.   Brodhead's discussion of Foucault notes that non-physical forms of discipline may be 'less visible but more pervasive' than corporal punishment (Brodhead, p 69). This development is evident not only in Victorian child-care literature but in Victorian children's literature, which emphasized the importance of the child's conscience as an internal monitor. Juvenile literature of the Georgian period depicted fear of punishment as the child's major motivation for good conduct; in contrast, 'deep earnestness, ... preoccupation with conscience, and ... heavy moral responsibilities imposed upon children' characterized Victorian juvenile literature until the advent of such non-didactic works as *Alice in Wonderland* in the 1860s (Avery, p. 64).

19.   See note 16.

20.   Several months after this incident, Mrs Gaskell noted with regret that Marianne had occasionally received a 'slight whipping' for obstinacy. The punishment was administered 'sorrowfully and gently, and has never failed in making her more obedient, without presenting the *least* resentful feeling' (p. 68). Although Gaskell seems to accept the necessity for these punishments, her uneasiness is evident in her emphasis upon the parents' gentleness and the child's supposed lack of resentment.

21.   Mrs Gaskell's letters include delightful glimpses of William enjoying their children through the years – flying a kite with Florence or teasing Julia about her impatience to open a present. 'He is very shy', Mrs Gaskell wrote after nearly thirty years of marriage, but 'very fond of children, playing with them all the day long ...' (*Letters*, no. 490, p. 660). William's affection for children was warmly recalled by Beatrix Potter, who was eight years old when she received a thank-you note from her elderly friend for the comforter she had knitted as a birthday gift. 'Big as I am, I know I could not have done it one-tenth as well', he assured her (letter qtd. in Uglow, pp. 612–13).

22.   In *Ruth*, the young mother is warned not to idolize her child, 'or God will, perhaps, punish you through him'. In *Sylvia's Lovers*, both parents adore their little daughter, but Gaskell's concern in this case is directed toward the husband's infatuation with his wife, whom he addresses, interestingly, as his 'child': 'I ha' made thee my idol; and, if I could live my life o'er again, I would love my God more, and thee less ...' (qtd. in Sharps, pp. 394–5).

23. Gaskell referred to Eddy Deane, whose father, Richard, was Dr Peter Holland's partner. Earlier in the diary, she wrote about another little boy who had died of croup and whose parents' devotion reminded her all too closely of her feelings for Marianne: 'Oh! how I trembled when I heard of it, and felt how insecure these "treasures in earthen vessels" are' (p. 63). Gaskell also described Marianne's frightening attack of croup in a letter to her sister-in-law, Lizzy Gaskell (*Letters*, no. 7, pp. 12–14). Marianne's crisis reappeared in one of Gaskell's first-published short stories 'Christmas Storms and Sunshine' (1848), in which a baby's attack of croup frightens a young mother.

24. See note 16.

25. *Ibid.*

26. A recently discovered letter, dated 15 March 1856, reveals that William, Jr., was not, as had been assumed, the Gaskells' only son. Writing to Harriet Carr Anderson, a friend who had long been out of touch, Mrs Gaskell mentioned 'the death of a little son while yet a baby' to account for the nearly six-year age gap between Meta and Florence. The baby must have died very shortly after birth; he was unnamed, and no other information about his brief existence has emerged to date. Neither the birth nor death was registered. In 'Two Unpublished Gaskell Letters', Chapple dates the birth between 1838 and 1841.

27. See note 16. These punishments were inflicted by Haldane's governess, albeit presumably with her parents' knowledge.

28. 'Miss F.' refers to Miss Fergusson, who was the children's nanny and then served as governess to Marianne and Meta. Mrs Gaskell was fond of her 'dear household friend' and cherished Miss Fergusson's kindness to Willie before his death (to Fanny Holland, 9 March 1847, qtd. in Uglow, p. 157). However, Gaskell reluctantly dismissed Miss Fergusson when it became apparent that she was unable to manage the older girls.

29. Edna Lyall's essay on Gaskell, published in 1897, includes passages from a letter by Marianne Gaskell Holland regarding her mother's life and achievements. Although Marianne recalled that her mother sometimes wrote 'late at night, when the house was quiet', neither the quoted excerpts from her letter nor Lyall's commentary acknowledge tension or conflict in Gaskell's balancing of multiple roles (qtd. by Lyall in Oliphant, p. 144). Lyall lauded Gaskell for taking 'a keen interest in the questions of the day' and for extending her sphere 'beyond the little world of home', while never allowing these activities to interfere with 'the noblest type' of family life (Lyall in Oliphant, p. 143). Gaskell's literary career was sanctioned by Lyall's fervent but oversimplified account of its origin as a heroic effort to overcome maternal grief.

30. Bonaparte's recent study interprets Gaskell's sobriquet as a symbolic key to a divided self, whose repressed rebellion against Victorian femininity created a 'subversive subtext' in her fiction (Bonaparte, p. 8): '... as always, through her humor Gaskell tells a serious truth ... Gaskell's words to Eliza Fox are especially astounding because they utterly annihilate the whole of "Mrs Gaskell's" existence. A bachelor does not have a family. A gypsy does not have a home' (Bonaparte, p. 218).

31. In 1849, Mary Howitt referred to Gaskell's 'many manuscripts which lie in a certain desk drawer, & may have lain there for years' (to Elizabeth Gaskell, 20 October 1849, qtd. in Uglow, p. 173).

32.   *Mary Barton* was not Gaskell's first venture into authorship. In 1838, she had written what Schor has termed 'audition letters' (*Letters*, nos. 8 and 12) to William and Mary Howitt, depicting scenes and incidents from her Knutsford childhood (Schor, p. 24). Her first published piece, 'Clopton Hall', described a girlhood visit to a mysterious old house and appeared in William Howitt's *Visits to Remarkable Places* (1840). By January 1848, Gaskell had three stories published in *Howitt's Journal*: 'Libbie Marsh's Three Eras', 'The Sexton's Hero', and 'Christmas Storms and Sunshine'. Her chosen pseudonym, 'Cotton Mather Mills', combined a pun on Manchester's industry with a hint of interest in Puritanism, which was later expressed in a story of the Salem witch trials, 'Lois the Witch' (1859). Uglow has suggested that 'Mather' resembles 'mother', and has noted that maternity is a central theme in Gaskell's first three published stories (Uglow, p. 172).

33.   This episode was supposedly based upon a visit which Gaskell made to a poor family in Manchester; as Uglow notes, the visit may have been actual or apocryphal (Uglow, p. 193).

34.   Quotations are from Maria Edgeworth's letter of 27 December 1848 to Mary Holland (qtd. in Easson, pp. 89–93).

35.   In his letter of December 1992, Alan Shelston raised a possible connection between the mysterious 'lost baby' and the cessation of Gaskell's diary. If she had been pregnant by October of 1838, she might have abandoned the diary due to the demands of pregnancy and not resumed it after the baby's death.

36.   Chapple has concluded that this letter, previously dated 1841, was written in 1840. Gaskell's feelings of depression and anxiety may have resulted from the death of her first son. See 'Two Unpublished Gaskell Letters'.

37.   Marianne was often called Polly or Minnie in Gaskell's letters. Meta was never called by her given name, Margaret; Florence was Flora or Flossy, and Elizabeth, to close friends and family, was Lily. Only William Sr. and Julia seem to have been without nicknames.

38.   Norton had previously met Gaskell and corresponded with her, but their meeting in Rome sparked a friendship which extended to Marianne and Meta after their mother's death. Norton belonged to a distinguished New England family and became a professor of art at Harvard, where his father had taught Biblical history and literature. Only 30 when he met the Gaskells in Italy, Norton became 'a pivotal figure in Anglo-American cultural relations' whose friends included Dickens, Browning, Darwin, Morris, Carlyle, George Eliot, Forster, and in America, Lowell, Longfellow, and Emerson (Bradley and Ousby, p. 86). In 1863, Gaskell dedicated the American edition of *Sylvia's Lovers* to Norton and his wife; their second daughter, born three years later, was named Elizabeth in honour of Mrs Gaskell (Uglow, pp. 417–21). Manuscripts of Meta Gaskell's letters to Norton are in the Houghton collection at Harvard.

39.   The title refers to an excerpt from Nightingale's *Cassandra*, an account of her intense dissatisfaction with conventional Victorian roles for women. She began the manuscript in 1852, but it was not published until 1928.

40.   Despite her displeasure, Gaskell gave Thurstan credit for his commitment to social justice. Along with several university friends, he pooled resources to build housing for the poor in London. '… it *is* a good & thoughtful thing of them to do', Gaskell acknowledged, '& I like to see that their previous luxurious (so to

speak) education has not unfitted them for strong feeling & prompt acting in behalf of those less fortunate' (*Letters*, no. 461, pp. 610–11).

41. With the help of Marianne, Thurstan and Meta, Gaskell had acquired a house in the country, keeping it a secret from William until the purchase was a *fait accompli*. In September 1865, Gaskell gleefully informed Charles Norton: '... I did a terribly grand thing! and a secret thing too! only you are in America and can't tell. I bought a house and 4 acres of land in Hampshire, – near Alton, – for Mr Gaskell to retire to & for a home for my unmarried daughters' (*Letters*, no. 583, p. 774). After Elizabeth's death, William chose to remain at the Plymouth Grove house in Manchester, where Meta and Julia continued to reside after their father's death in 1884.

42. Ann Hearn joined the Gaskell household as a young servant and nurse in 1842. Hearn, as she was always known, remained as a beloved and indispensable member of the family for over fifty years. She and the Gaskells looked after each other with mutual devotion. 'She is a dear good valuable *friend*', Mrs Gaskell declared (*Letters*, no. 570, p. 760).

43. Thurstan's letter to Charles Norton, dated 18 November 1865, is reprinted in Chapple and Pollard, *Letters*, pp. 970–71, from a copy in the Princeton University Library. Cuts, here marked by ellipses within brackets, were made by the copyist.

Persons and places

Elizabeth Stevenson (1810–65) was married to the Reverend William Gaskell (1805–84), junior minister at Cross Street Unitarian chapel in Manchester, in 1832. They went to live at No. 1 Dover Street, Oxford Road, on what was then the southern edge of the city. About fifteen miles further south was Knutsford in Cheshire, where Elizabeth's maternal aunt, Hannah Lumb (1767–1837), had brought her up from babyhood. Mrs Lumb, a widow from 1805, seems to have been sharing a house at Heathside with her only living sister, Abigail Holland (1773–1848), about the time the diary was written. In May 1836 Elizabeth and her daughter Marianne (1834–1920) went to stay a few miles away from Knutsford at the old family home of her grandparents, Sandle-bridge Farm (*Letters,* no. 4, p. 5). Mrs Lumb died on 1 May 1837.

Bessy (1796–1886) was a daughter by his first wife of Mrs Lumb's brother Dr Peter Holland (1766–1855), who had inherited Sandlebridge in 1816. When the Gaskells went to Wales in September 1837, Bessy looked after Marianne, and their second daughter Meta (1837–1913) was cared for by Mrs Mary Ann Deane, wife of Peter Holland's partner, Dr Richard Thomas Deane. Two of their five children are mentioned in the diary: Edward, who was born in December 1833 but died in 1838 (*Letters,* nos. 3 and 7, pp. 4, 13), and Emily, who was born in 1835 and still living in 1861. Mrs Deane died on 30 March 1842, aged 30, and Richard married Bessy Holland's younger half-sister, Susan (1811–1889) on 10 April 1844. Richard himself died on 20 January 1851, aged 46.

Aunt Anne (1797–?1851) was the oldest daughter of Samuel Holland (1768–1851), a younger brother of Dr Peter Holland. Samuel's family lived at Toxteth Park, Liverpool, and later at Plas yn Penrhyn, near Porthmadog in North Wales, where the Gaskells spent part of their honeymoon. In the summer of 1836 Anne was staying with Mrs Gaskell at Grange-over-Sands, a Cumbrian resort on Morecambe Bay opposite Silverdale. Crosby is also on this coast but further south, only just north of Liverpool.

At Sankey Street, Warrington, a town between Liverpool and Manchester, lived William Gaskell's mother, Margaret, who died on 12 January 1850 aged 69. After the death of her husband in 1819, she had made a second marriage to the Reverend Edward R. Dimock, minister of the Unitarian chapel in the centre of the town from 1822 to 1841.

William's brother Samuel (1807–86) became a doctor and practised for a time (1832–40) in Manchester and nearby Stockport. Family ties were strengthened in 1838 when the younger sister of William and Samuel Gaskell, Elizabeth (1812–92), married Charles (1799–1870), eldest son of Samuel Holland. James E. Partington, who also looked after the family of the Reverend J. G. Robberds, William Gaskell's senior colleague at Cross Street chapel, was a surgeon of Oxford Road, Manchester.

Prospect Hill was a large house in the country south of Warrington owned by Holbrook Gaskell (1771–1842). He had married another Gaskell, Ann, William's paternal aunt; they had no children. William was left a legacy in her will of 1848. Another nephew, Holbrook Gaskell (1813–1909), to whom the property had been bequeathed, took up residence at Prospect Hill in 1850. The Collins family, possibly of Manchester, occurs in *Letters*, nos. 9 and 11, pp. 18, 25. The surnames of servants mentioned in the diary are not known.

The diary

To my dear little Marianne I shall 'dedicate' this book, which, if I should not live to give it her myself, will I trust be reserved for her as a token of her mother's love, and extreme anxiety in the formation of her little daughter's character. If that little daughter should in time become a mother herself, she may take an interest in the experience of another; and at any rate she will perhaps like to become acquainted with her character in it's [*sic*] earliest form. I wish that (if ever she sees this) I could give her the slightest idea of the love and the hope that is bound up in her. The love which passeth every earthly love, and the hope that however we may be separated on earth, we may each of us so behave while sojourning here that we may meet again to renew the dear & tender tie of Mother and Daughter.[1]

March 10th Tuesday Evening. 1835.
    The day after tomorrow Marianne will be six months old. I wish I had begun my little journal sooner, for (though I should have laughed at the idea twelve months ago) there have been many little indications of disposition &c. already; which I can not now remember clearly. I will try and describe her *mentally*. I should call her remarkably good tempered; though at time she gives way to little bursts of passion or perhaps impatience would be the right name. She is also very firm in her own little way occasionally; what I suppose is obstinacy really, only that is so hard a word to apply to one so dear. But in general she is so good that I feel as if I could hardly be sufficiently thankful, that the materials put into my hands are so excellent, and beautiful. And yet it seems to increase the responsibility. If I should misguide from carelessness or negligence! *wilfully* is not in a mother's heart. From ignorance and errors in judgement I know I may, and probably shall, very often. But oh Lord I pray thee to lead me right (if it be thy will) and to preserve in me the same strong feeling of my responsibility which I now feel. And you too my dearest little girl, if when you read this, you trace back any evil, or unhappy feeling to my mismanagement in your childhood forgive me, love!
    Marianne is now becoming every day more and more interesting. She

looks at and tries to take hold of everything. She has pretty good ideas of distance and does not try to catch sunbeams now, as she did two months ago. Her sense of sight is much improved lately in seeing objects at a distance, and distinguishing them. For instance I had her in my arms today in the drawing-room, and her Papa was going out of the gate, and she evidently knew him; smiled and kicked. She begins to show a decided preference to those she likes; she puts out her little arms to come to me, and would I am sure, do so to her Papa. She catches the expression of a countenance to which she is accustomed directly; when we laugh, she laughs; and when I look attentive to William's reading, it is quite ridiculous to see her little face of gravity, and earnestness, as if she understood every word. I try always to let her look at anything which attracts her notice as long she will, and when I see her looking very intently at anything, I take her to it, and let her exercise all her senses upon it – even to tasting, if I am sure it can do her no harm. My object is to give her a habit of fixing her attention.

She takes great delight in motion just at present; dancing, jumping, shutting and opening the hand pleases her very much. I had no idea children at her age, made such continued noises; she shouts, and murmurs, and talks in her way, just like conversation, varying her tones &c. I wish we could know what is passing in her little mind. She likes anything like singing, but seems afraid of the piano; today she even began to cry, when I began to play. In general I think she is remarkably free from fear or shyness of any sort. She goes to any one who will take her. Staring at strangers to be sure, and being very grave while they are in the room, but not crying, or clinging to me. I am very glad of this, as though it is very flattering and endearing to me, yet I should be sorry if she were to get the habit of refusing to go to others.

Then as to her 'bodily' qualifications, she has two teeth cut with very little trouble; but I believe the worst are to come. She is very strong in her limbs, though because she is so fat, we do not let her use her ancles at all, and I hope she will be rather late in walking that her little legs may be very firm. I shall find it difficult to damp the energies of the servants in this respect, but I intend that she shall teach herself to walk, & receive no assistance from hands &c. She lies down on the floor a good deal, and kicks about; a practice I began very early, and which has done her a great deal of good. She goes to bed *awake*; another practice I began early, and which is so comfortable I wonder it is not more generally adopted. Once or twice we have had grand cryings, which have been very very distressing to me; but when I have convinced myself that she is not in pain, is perfectly well, and that she is only wanting to be taken up I have been quite firm, though I have sometimes cried almost as much as she has. I never leave her till she is asleep (except in extreme cases) and as she is put to bed at a regular time (6 o'clock) she generally gets very sleepy while being undressed. While the undressing is going on, I never like her to be talked to, played with, or excited yet sometimes she is so very playful when she ought to be put down, that a turn or two up and down the room is required to soothe her, still putting her down awake. Sometimes she will cry a little, and when I turn her over in her cot she fancies she is going to be taken up and is still in a moment making the peculiar little triumphing noise she always does when she is pleased.

Crying has been a great difficulty with me. Books do so differ. One says 'Do not let them have anything they cry for', another (Mme Neckar de Saussure, sur L'Education Progressive, the nicest book I have read on the subject) says 'les larmes des enfans [sic] sont si amères, la calme parfaite de l'âme leur est si necessaire [sic] qu'il faut surtout épargner des larmes.' So I had to make a rule for myself, and though I am afraid I have not kept to it quite as I ought, I still think it a good one. We must consider that a cry is a child's only language for expressing its wants. It is its little way of saying, 'I am hungry. I am very cold,' and *so*, I don't think we should carry out the maxim of never letting a child have anything for crying. If it is to have the object for which it is crying I would give it, it, *directly*, giving up any little occupation or purpose of my own, rather than try its patience *unnecessarily*. But if it is improper for it to obtain the object, I think it right to with-hold it steadily, however much the little creature may cry. I think after one or two attempts to conquer by crying the child would become aware that *one* cry or indication of a want was sufficient, and I think the habit of crying would be broken. I am almost sure even my partial adherence to this plan has prevented many crying fits with Marianne. I have somewhere read that a child gets bad habits, *first by being irritated* and then by finding that crying causes the irritation to cease. I think this is very true. I think it is the duty of every mother to sacrifice a good deal rather than have her child *unnecessarily* irritated by anything – food given irregularly or improperly, dress uncomfortable, even to an uneasy position. I think this rule should be attended to. But though I keep laying down rules, I fear I have not sufficiently attended to them, though I hope I have been conscientious hitherto in discharging my duty to her. Still I sometimes fear there is too much pride in my own heart in attributing her goodness to the success of my plans, when in reality it is owing to her having hitherto had such good health, and freedom from pain, a blessing for which I can not be too thankful. Still I put down everything now because I have thought a good deal about the formation of any little plans, and I shall like to know their success. I want to act on principles *now*[2] which can be carried on through the whole of her education. I have written a great deal tonight, and very unconnectedly. I had no idea the journal of my own disposition, & feelings was so intimately connected with that of my little baby, whose regular breathing has been the music of my thoughts all the time I have been writing. God bless her.

August 4th Tuesday Evening. 1835.

It seems a very long time since I have written anything about my little darling, and I feel as if I had been negligent about it, only it is so difficult to know when to begin or when to stop when talking thinking or writing about her.

In a few days she will be eleven months old; and in some things I suppose she is rather backward; in walking and talking for instance. *I* fancy she says Mama, but I think it is only fancy. She can stand pretty steadily, taking hold of something, for a few minutes and then she pops down. But as I am not very anxious for her to walk or talk earlier than her nature prompts, and as her Papa thinks the same, we allow her to take her own way.

She has various little accomplishments of her own, clapping hands, shaking hands, which are very pretty, though I sometimes fear we rather try to make her exhibit too much to strangers. We must take care of this as she grows older. She understands many words & sentences 'Where are the cows', 'the flies' &c &c &c. I am very much afraid of her catching cross or angry expressions of countenance or even one that is not quite happy. I find her own changes so directly to the expression she sees. If we[3] could but consider a child properly, what a beautiful safe-guard from evil would it's presence be. Oh! I do hope & intend …

[A portion of the leaf is cut away at this point. About six lines missing]

How all a woman's life, at least so it seems to me now, ought to have a reference to the period when she will be fulfilling one of her greatest & highest duties, those of a mother. I feel myself so unknowing, so doubtful about many things in her intellectual & moral treatment already, and what shall I be when she grows older, & asks those puzzling questions that children do? I hope I shall always preserve my present good intentions & sense of my holy trust, and then I must pray, to be forgiven for my errors, & led into a better course.

[About six lines missing]

… afraid of pleasure being associated with the faces of pain they pull. Perhaps this is foolish but I will put everything down relating to her.

She has been to Knutsford and Warrington since I last wrote in this journal. And oh! after her visit to Warrington she was very very ill; and I was very much afraid we should have lost her. I did so try to be resigned; but I cannot tell how I sickened at my heart, at the thought of seeing her no more here.

> Her empty crib to see
> Her silent nursery,
> Once gladsome with her mirth.

I am sometimes afraid of using expressions of gratitude to God, for fear I should get into the habit of using them, without sufficiently feeling them, but I think there is no danger when I say that I bless & thank my Father, & hers, for not taking away the blessing he gave; and oh! may I not make her into an idol, but strive to prepare both her & myself for the change that may come any day.

After her illness her temper had suffered from the indulgence that was necessary during her illness; but as she grew strong it wore away, and I think she is now as sweet-tempered as ever in general; though at times her little passions are terrible and give me quite a heavy heart.

I should say impatience will be one of her greatest faults; and I scarcely knows [sic] the best way of managing it. I certainly think being calm one-self & showing that her impatience makes no difference in the quickness or slowness of her actions, and never disappointing her when *unnecessary* are good rules; but then in every little case it is so difficult for an unde-cided person like me to determine at once, and yet *every body* & every book says that decision is of such consequence to the comfort & conse-quently to the temper of a child; & that it is almost better for *the time*, to go on with a treatment that is *not bad*, rather than by changing to a better, let the child see your wavering. I only mean for the time. I must take care to have presence of mind to remark & adopt the better method every future occasion.

There is another thing I try to attend to & make the servants attend to; more by way of distracting her attention to call it to a thing that is not there, and never to promise her anything unconditionally without performing it.

Of course she now knows all those whom she is in the habit of seeing. I do not think she is remarkably shy, although more so than she was. But certainly most people take children in such a brusque injudicious manner that no wonder they are often shy.

And now I shall conclude tonight, & I do not intend to be so long again without writing about my dear little girl.

Sunday Evening Augus⁴ October 4 1835

I see it is exactly two months since I last wrote in this book, and I hope my little girl is improved both in 'body & mind' since then. She suffered a good deal from the changes of weather we have had, and I have found it necessary to leave off milk as an article of diet at present. She lives on broth thickened with arrowroot, & I think this food strengthens her, but she is still a delicate child, and backward in walking. I hope she will not be hurried by any one in her attempts at trotting about, for the more I see and hear of children the more I am convinced that when they feel their limbs strong enough to begin to walk they will constantly be trying their pow-ers, & that till Nature prompts this, it is worse than useless to force them to their feet.

She is I believe a small child of her age, though tall, and she has looked (& been too, alas!) very delicate since that sad, sad illness in the summer.

I am going to clothe her in flannel waist-coats, and long sleeves to her frocks this winter, and to keep her in *well-aired* rooms in preference to going much out of doors unless the weather is very tempting. She has now had eight teeth for some time, and is about some more I fancy; perhaps when her teeth are all through her health may be stronger. Oh may I try not to fasten & centre my affections too strongly on such a frail little treasure, but all my anxiety though it renders me so aware of her fragility of life makes me cling daily more & more to her.

I think her disposition has improved since I wrote last; she is not so impatient (perhaps it was the remains of her former illness.) She does not throw herself back in the passionate way she used to do seven or eight weeks ago, and she bears her little disappointments better. The fewer she can have of these, & the better I think, and I try to avoid exciting her expectations, even when they are pretty certain of being gratified, for the excitement (which is always so great in a child) is injurious, & produces a degree of impatience. There are & always will be enow of disappointments to enure a child to bearing them, and they will encrease with years and with the power of enduring, & what I mean to say is that all that can be averted by a little fore-thought on the part of the parent or nurse, without interfering with the necessary degree of quiet but resolute discipline, should be attended to and removed. I do not like the plan in fashion formerly, of *making* trials for young children; there will naturally be some which the child must bear, and the parent calmly witness, but creating disappointments on purpose to enure the poor little things to them in after-life seems like giving them rich unsuitable food, which grown up people may & do eat, but which their delicate stomachs cannot yet digest. When young their feelings, especially those under the direct control of the senses are so acute, while the powers which will eventually it is to be hoped, control their feeling are in a dormant state.

It is quite astonishing to see the difference bodily feelings make in Marianne's temper & powers of endurance. I was in a great measure prepared for this by Combe's Physiology, but I had no idea how every change of temper might be deduced from some corresponding change in the body. Mothers are sometimes laughed at for attributing little freaks of temper to teething &c, but I don't think those who laugh at them (I used to be one) have had much to do with children. I do not mean to say that the habit of self control may not be given and that at a very early age, but I think that with certain states of the body, feelings will arise which *ought* to be controlled, and that everything physical tending to produce those peculiar states of the body should be avoided, with as much care as we would avoid anything moral tending to produce moral evil. I wish I could act more upon this conviction myself; want of sleep invariably brings on an irritable state of excitement; and want of food, though I may not have the sensation of hunger, has in general the same effect.

I should describe Marianne as a child with whom excitement should be particularly avoided; and yet it is a very tempting thing to see the little cheek flush, & the eye dilate, and the childish lip look so eloquent. She is very much tired & consequently more irritable after a certain degree of play, & novelty, and besides her sensibilities seem to me very acute. If she sees others laughing when she is grave & serious, or is not aware of the joke; she bursts into tears; I fancy it must [be] a want of sympathy with her (at the time) serious & thoughtful feelings which makes her cry, but it must be a morbid feeling I should think, & one that for her happiness had better be checked, *if I but knew how*. Then unexpected pleasure has occasionally made her cry; seeing her Papa after an absence of a few days; and I thought tears were not a common manifestation of joy in children (so young, not 13 months old yet[)]. I feel very ignorant of the best way of managing these sensibilities, so beautiful when healthy, & so distressing when morbid. Perhaps as her body becomes stronger, her mind will too. There is a laugh of hers which is almost sure to end in a cry. She is in general very gentle, rather grave especially with strangers, and remarkably observing, watching actions, things &c with such continued attention. She is very *feminine* I think in her quietness which is as far removed from inactivity of mind as possible. She sits on the ground much more than she did, amusing herself pretty well (this amusing *herself*, has been I fear more my theory than my practice). I do not think she shows much perseverance, otherwise she would try longer to reach her playthings herself &c, but this *may be* bodily instability.

Her accomplishments are numerous and varied; – barking like a dog, mewing, *in a way*, kissing, pointing to various articles when named &c &c &c.

William told me the other day I was not of a jealous disposition; I do not think he knows me; in general Marianne prefers being with me I hope & think, yet at times she shows a marked preference for Betsy, who has always been as far as I can judge a kind, judicious, and tender nurse. Tonight Marianne was sadly tired, and I would fain have caressed & soothed her while Betsy was performing various little offices for her on her knee, and MA absolutely pushed me away, fearing I should take her. This was hard to bear; but I am almost sure I have never shown this feeling to any one; for I believe Betsy fully deserves and returns her love, & having more bodily strength can amuse her more than I can in different ways. There will come a time when she will know how a mother's love exceeds all others; & meanwhile, I will try never to put myself in rivalry with another for my childs affections but to encourage very good & grateful feeling on her part towards every one; and particularly towards a faithful & affectionate servant.

I have been much gratified these few days past by the beginning of self restraint in the little creature; she has sometime been washed in water either too hot, or too cold, and taken a dislike to it. This week past I have in general got up to wash her myself, or see by the thermometer that the water was the right heat (from 85 to 90) and Betsy and I have tried to distract her attention & prevent her crying; this last two days she has tried hard to prevent herself from crying, giving gulps & strains to keep it down. Oh may this indeed be the beginning of self-government!

Lord! unto thee do I commit this darling precious treasure; thou knowest how I love her; I pray that I may not make her too much my idol; and oh! if thou shouldst call her away from 'the evil to come' may I try to yield her up to him who gave her to me without a murmur. I hope I may say thou also knowest how truly I wish to do my duty to her; Help my ignorance O Lord strengthen my good purposes, & preserve a due sense of my holy trust, which I now acknowledge with fear & trembling; And yet if I do right in endeavouring, thou Lord wilt bless me and her, and lead her right at last, and forgive her mother's errors. I pray thee to bless her through our Lord Jesus Christ.

Monday Evening Decr 28. 1835.

My darling little girl! how long it is since I wrote about you. But I have been ill, and perhaps lazy, which I certainly ought not to be in anything concerning you.

Marianne is much stronger I trust than when I wrote last, but she has required a great deal of care, & very nourishing food; isinglass dissolved in broth &c. With her strength has her good temper returned, which is in accordance with my theory that when *children* at any rate, are irritable something is physically the matter with them. When she does become angry now, she is easily calmed, and we have begun to try and make her show sorrow – it can be but showing at present; but when she has been angry, we look grave (*not angry*) & sometimes put our hands before our faces, which always attracts her attention & by so doing stops her little passion. She tries to pull in [sic] down, & I generally ask her 'is Baby sorry for having been impatient &c'; which she quite understands, and in general makes her little assenting noise, & kisses me. She quite understands me when I gently tell her to be patient about anything. 'Wait a little bit dear little Baby; Betsy will come soon', always makes her still; because for one thing, I have never allowed her to be told any one was going to do anything for her, unless they *really* were, and have tried to speak as *truly* to her as ever I could. If before Betsy comes with her dinner or whatever she wants, she again becomes fidgetty I again ask her to wait, and show her something to amuse her. When she is hurt she seldom cries much, and if she does we show her something, a picture a glass a book, & she directly forgets it. We *show* our pity as little as we can.

She is not greedy though often very hungry; but I think at any time she likes us to have a piece, or a spoonful of whatever she is having, provided we do not take it out of her hand, which we do not attempt to do, as a trustful spirit on her part can not be made by violence, but will come naturally when she sees that we are scrupulous in respecting her little rights. A few weeks ago her Grandmama sent her some sweet biscuits, and at first I feared she was inclined to be selfish with these luxuries, for she had never tasted anything sweet before. She refused occasionally when we asked for a bit, instead of offering with her own accord, but it wore off, and now she gives as freely as ever.

She is remarkably good in being content with a refusal, if we do not think any eatable proper for her. She kisses, & points & tries to speak, but does not cry when we say no. I speak in general for of course there are times when she is not so good. Her greatest naughtiness is in being washed & dressed. She cries sadly over the washing which I think must be owing to her having been put in it[5] too cold some time. She dislikes *finishing* her food, and by an curious sort of fancy, often refuses the last two or three spoonsful through dread of coming to the bottom.

I am rather afraid from being the only child, she is a little too dependent on others, for instance if when sitting on the floor a plaything rolls away, she has no idea of scrambling after it, but looks up beseechingly for someone to help her. To be sure she is very weak in her limbs scarcely attempting to walk with two hands, though nearly 16 months.

She is extremely fond of her Papa, shouting out his name whenever she hears his footstep, never mistaking it, and dancing with delight when she hears the bell which is a signal for her to come in after dinner.

She will talk before she walks I think. She can say pretty plainly 'Papa, dark stir, ship, lamp, book, tea, sweep' &c – leaving poor *Mama* in the back ground. She is delighted when we stir the fire or make any *commotion* in the room. I am sometimes surprized to find how she understands, & tries to understand what we say amongst ourselves.

For instance I was one day speaking of *biscuits*, but fearing if she understood me, her hopes would be excited, I merely described them as 'things that were on the breakfast-table this morning'. (There were none in[6] the room at the time, when immediately she began to dance in Fanny's arms saying Bis, bis, bis. She is I think a small child, & I fear not a very strong one. We hope to take her to the sea-side this spring. Oh may I constantly bear in mind the words 'The Lord hath given, & the Lord hath taken away. Blessed be the name of the Lord.' I feel weak & exhausted with writing, or I had meant to write more. God bless my dearest child, and help her mother in her earnest endeavours.

Febry 7th 1836.

This morning we heard a sermon from the text 'And his mother kept all these sayings in her heart'. Oh! how very, very true it is – and

I sometimes think I may find this little journal a great help in recalling the memory of my darling child, if we should lose her.

We have had much cause for thankfulness since I wrote last; she has daily improved in health, and I think her character has developed itself a good deal latterly, and promises to be amiable & affectionate. I see I have generally begun my journal with describing the bodily progress she has made, and I will keep to the proper order of things. She can manage to walk by herself with the assistance of chairs, the sofa &c. and the natural consequence of this exercise of the muscles of her legs is that they have become more developed & consequently stronger; indeed her whole body bespeaks her a more healthy child. There is that mottled look on the flesh, which gives such joy to a mother's eye. She has eight single, and four double teeth, and suffers *comparatively* little when she cuts them. There is loss of spirits & appetite, but no fits, or even fever, and spirits & appetite come back, & bring their attendant good-humour when the cause is removed. She has a colour like a cherry, instead of the flushed warning red it used to be; and certainly with health, beauty has come; and I confess I think beauty a desirable thing. True like most other gifts it has its temptations, but still it is a high gift in the influence it irresistibly gives its possessor over others – an influence which may be used for such noble purposes.

In general she is very sweet-tempered – true there are little bursts of passion which will require watchfulness & care, but she soon puts up her finger, and says 'hush' & offers to kiss the person she has offended against. Another more difficult *fault*? is her disobedience – She does not seem at present to have an idea of obedience; she is very obliging and will often do the thing we desire her to do, but sometimes she resists very merrily & in good-temper – puzzling me sadly as to the right course to take. For instance when she come near a great gap between two chairs, I call to her to come back to Mama; she laughs and still goes on; in general I get up and take her up, & set her down at her starting point, when she begins again, quite good-tempered. Once or twice I have let her go on, & she has had a slight tumble which I have tried to tell her was in consequence of disobeying Mama –

She is very affectionate; when I am poorly, or whenever she thinks any one is hurt or sorry, she strokes their faces, saying 'poor Mama, poor Papa &c' – Her great delight just now is in make-believe letters; reading her one from Aunt Lumb, and introducing the names of all the things she knows, such as 'flowers, geese &c.['] This and pictures delight her extremely, but certainly she is not so independent as she should be, and as I intended her to be. She has not much idea of amusing herself, which has been a great error in her education hitherto, probably issuing from her delicacy in part. She is remarkably fond of children, and I am glad to give her an oppy of gratifying this fondness by taking her this week to stay a day or two at Mrs Collins, who has a little girl five or six months younger than Marianne. She seems to have a good memory, and good natural talents; I hope they may never be neglected through me.

Lord thou knowest that the 'sin that doth so easily beset me' hath overtaken me once or twice even with this dear child – but thou knowest too how bitterly I have repented, and how earnestly I mean to try for the future. Help thou my weakness, Oh Lord, and bless my endeavours to conquer myself, and oh above all things may her presence be as holy to me, checking each angry word that might injure the precious soul which thou hast given to this little child. Bless her, and bless her mother, who in sorrow confesses her fault and prays for thy guidance in her future conduct. Oh Lord God Almighty bless my child, as thou seest fit & best for her, but may she hear the glad words when her mortal life is done, 'Well done good & faithful servant, enter thou into the joy of thy Lord'.

Novr 5th 1836.

The greater part of this summer has been passed in rather an unsettled way, what with visits to Knutsford, Warrington and to the sea-side, and I fear this is the only excuse I have for so long neglecting to enter anything in my journal. A great progress has naturally been made by the dear little subject since writing last. I do not think her health has had any material draw-back though for some time her languor in attempting to walk caused me some uneasiness. When we were at Knutsford (in May) Mr Deane quite forbid her being put upon her feet and the consequence of course was that she lost the little idea of walking which she had before. At Prospect Hill she gained strength though she had one violent attack, (beginning with violent screaming as if in pain), but we put her directly into warm water, & gave her castor oil, sending at the same time for a medical man, who decided that the inflammatory state of her body was owing to her being on the point of cutting her eye-teeth. He said the course I had pursued before he came was decidedly the best and safest in all sudden attacks with children. After these said eye-teeth came through, or to speak *very* exactly in the beginning of July 1836, when she was two and twenty months old, she began almost suddenly to walk by herself, and since then her bodily strength has come on very much indeed. For some time, indeed even now we are very careful to comply with her request to be taken 'up, up', when she is tired of walking, as I think the exercise gives her such a pleasurable feeling, that it must be fatigue and not caprice that lead her to ask to be carried. She is very careful and has a good idea of danger; not like some children who have been forced rather too early to their feet and seem not to be able to measure distances. So much for her feats in the walking line. She has now 16 teeth, and we think she is cutting her back double teeth, but as these give comparatively little pain I do not feel anxious about them. I have often intended to measure her height, but somehow or other it has hitherto slipped through; but from her frocks I guess she has grown a good deal these last eight weeks, and good need she had of it, for she was a little rolly-polly before.

She is a famous chatter-box seldom letting her little tongue rest either with sense or nonsense, and it is amusing to hear her talk in this latter fashion, inventing so many new sounds in such varied tones. Her great delight is in hearing 'tories', and little scraps of verse; and I think she shows a pretty good memory in repeating them again. We have not begun yet to teach her anything feeling in no hurry to urge her little capacity forward, and in this we have been in many ways confirmed. We heard the opinion of a medical man lately, who said that till the age of three years or thereabouts, the brain of an infant appeared constantly to be verging on inflammation, which any *little*[7] excess of excitement might produce. If we give her habits of observation, attention & perseverance, in *whatever* objects her little mind may be occupied with, I shall think we are laying a good foundation, and four years old will be time enough to begin with *lessons* &c, & even then it shall be in compliance with her own wish to learn, which wish I must try to excite. So much for *intellect*. Now for morals.

There have been times when I have felt, oh! so cast down by her wrong-doing, and as I think I am very easily impressible, I have fancied there must have been some great mismanagement to produce such little obstinate fits, and whole hours of wilfulness. I do not however think that this has been often the case, and when it has, my cooler judgement has been aware of some little circumstance connected with her physical state that has in some measure accounted for it. For instance, she, (like her mother) requires a great deal of sleep. She is *always* in bed, and asleep by seven, frequently earlier, and seldom wakens before six at the earliest. Then she requires from two to three hours sleep in the middle of the day, and if by any chance her time for sleep goes by she is weary, fretful and as unlike the merry happy little creature she is in general as possible. We have been puzzled for a punishment. The usual one, putting the little offender into a corner had no effect with her, as she made it into a game to 'I[8] *do* into a corner and be naughty little girl'; so the last we have tried is putting her into a high chair, from which she cannot get out, and leaving her there (always in the same room with one of us) till some little sign of sorrow is shown. This with grave and sorrowful looks on our part has generally had the desired effect. She often talks to herself about the consequences of her conduct. 'Baby *dood dirl*, make Papa and Mama happy.' 'Baby not dood dirl, Papa & Mama so sorry,' &c. I think for so young a child she has a pretty correct idea as to whether actions are right or wrong. We had an instance lately when *some one*, in anger did what was decidedly wrong in her presence, without considering how holy that little creature made the place. She took no notice, at the time but the next morning

told me of it, adding 'that *was* naughty'. Though much interested in preserving her love and respect for the person to whom I allude, I knew it
was my duty not to weaken her power of discriminating, & said 'it was
very naughty, but she was very sorry now &c.'

A few weeks ago she got a habit of refusing her food, saying 'bye-bye'
&c when a spoonful was offered to her which she did not quite approve.
I found the best plan was to take her at her word, and quietly send the
plate away, which at first produced sad fits of crying, and throwing herself
back but after once or twice she became less saucy, and takes her food
very pleasantly now. I think she is not a greedy child, whatever her other
faults may be. She knows when she has had enough. She gave me a very
pretty little instance of unselfishness when we were last at Knutsford
which pleased me very much. We were calling at Mrs Deanes who has two
children, one about 9 months older, the other about that much younger
than Marianne. A few comfits were thrown on the carpet, which the
youngest child (little Emily) could hardly manage to pick up. My own
dear Marianne however did not put one into her own mouth, though as
fond of them as could be, but crammed them into little Emily. It made
my heart glad.

I am not aware that any promise has been made to her that has not
been strictly fulfilled. And the consequence is she has a firm reliance on
our word, and a pretty good idea of giving up a present pleasure to secure
a future one, feeling sure that the promise will be performed. While at
Grange it was necessary for her to bathe, and I dreaded it for her.
Luckily her Aunt Anne a capital bather was with us, and undertook the
charge of her, which was so much better than being frightened by being
given over to a strange woman in an uncouth dress. We made the period
of suspense as short as possible, undressing her directly, and giving her,
her plunges immediately. I stood on the rocks with a shawl ready to
receive her & give her a biscuit; & though she often said while being
undressed 'Baby not bathe Mama', we never had any crying or screaming. She has lately had occasion to take one or two doses of Epsom Salts,
and I have always told her beforehand they were bad bad, but were to
do her good, & she has taken them directly, looking however strongly
inclined to cry when the cup is taken from her lips, but a biscuit as a
reward soon puts a stop to this. Sometimes as a proof of our pleasure we
have given her a spunge biscuit, ½ a doz comfits, or a bit of Pomfret Cake,
but we try not to make her expect these things, which are only occasional but to depend for her reward on our pleased countenances and
expressions, and our willingness to play and romp with her. This love of
an earthly parent's approbation we hope in time to lead into a higher
feeling.

A few weeks since she saw the funeral of a young girl in her walk
with Betsy, and showing in her way some curiosity on the subject, Betsy

injudiciously but very naturally told her it was a poor girl that they were going to put into a hole and cover her up with earth. This made a great impression on her. Once or twice when she has been awakened in the night, she has so directly recurred to it with signs of affright, that we have concluded she has been dreaming of it, and we have done our best to counteract the feelings excited by telling her the girl was very happy, and was gone to *bi-bi* &c.

She is very touching in her sweet little marks of affection. Once or twice when I have seemed unhappy about little things she has come and held up her sweet mouth to be kissed. Last night I was in pain, & made a sort of moan. She was lying by me apparently asleep, but as if her gentle instinct of love prompted her even then, she pressed to me, saying 'Kiss, Mama'. These are trifles but how very precious may the remembrance of them become. We yesterday heard of a connexion of William's who had just lost his only child a fine lad of nine or ten by a sudden attack of croup. His father and mother were wrapped in the boy, who had every promise of excellence. Oh! how I trembled when I heard of it, and felt how insecure these 'treasures in earthen vessels' are.

Oh God! give me that spirit which can feel and say not my will but thine be done. Teach me to love this darling child with perfect submission to thy decrees. I dare hardly think of the uncertain future, but thou wilt uphold me in time of trial; and into thy hands I commit my treasure. Do with her Oh Lord as seemeth best unto thee, for thou art a God of Love & wilt not causelessly afflict. Bless her in every way I earnestly beseech thee, through Jesus Christ our Lord.

December 9th 1837
I feel quite ashamed to see that more than a year has passed since I last wrote. There have been some sad excuses to be sure. I had very bad health till my dear little Meta was born, February 5th 1837, and I had hardly recovered my strength when (March 10th) I received a summons to Knutsford. My dearest Aunt Lumb, my more than mother had had a paralytic stroke on Wednesday March 8th; For eight weeks I remained in lodgings at Knutsford, with my two little girls, and our dear servant Betsy; and on May 1st I lost my best friend. May God reward her for all her kindness to me.

After that I was much out of health for some time and went to Crosby in July. In September William and I went into Wales for three weeks, leaving Marianne with Bessy Holland, and Meta with Mrs Deane. We have lost our servant Betsy, who was obliged to leave us, being wanted at home, in consequence of the death of a sister. But we still keep her as a friend, and she has been to stay with us several weeks this autumn. Her place is supplied by Elizabeth, a clever servant, and who is very kind to the children especially to little Meta. I have given this little account of the changes in our domestic relations, that if this book be given to Marianne, (as I hope it will be) after my death she may understand more fully anything I may have occasion to allude to.

When my most dearly loved Aunt left this house for the last time, (Janry 15th 1837) she took Marianne back with her to Knutsford; to stay with her over the time of my approaching confinement. As Aunt Lumb's eyesight had failed her very much, she was unable to write; so I had no particular accounts of my darling; only general news of her health. But since, I have asked my cousins &c to tell me all the particulars of the seven weeks that MA staid with Aunt Lumb before she was seized with her last illness. They say, that Aunt Lumb seemed so very fond of 'her little Marianne'. One day some one met my Aunt out of doors; – she had been about an hour out, and said she was hastening home, for she did not think she had left MA so long before; The little girl slept in a cot by Aunt Lumb's bed; Aunt Lumb gave her, her breakfast, sitting on her knee, by a window, with many loving little jokes between them. Aunt Lumb walked out with her, when the weather permitted. And it was to Aunt Lumb, that Marianne ran when in any little distress; and to her that she always clung.

The very day Aunt Lumb was seized with her fatal attack, she had been with Marianne in Mrs Deane's poney-carriage to the Infant-school, and was so pleased with Marianne's pleasure.

That evening about ½ past 10, she had a paralytic stroke. MA was as usual in her little sofa bed by Aunt Lumb's, and remained there till morning, when she wanted according to her custom to come into Aunt Lumb's bed. But Aunt Lumb did not heed the little voice that kept petitioning to be taken in, and when they told her 'Aunt Lumb was poorly' she kept saying 'Aunt Lumb tell me if you are poorly'. Of course she was sent to a friend's till I came.

We were confined to two little bed-rooms in that unhappy eight weeks, and the little girls could hardly ever go out. But Marianne was a good little comfort, though in such trying circumstances to a child's temper. Aunt Lumb asked to see her, about a week after her first seizure; and I took MA in. But the room was darkened gloomy [sic]; Aunt Lumb had had leeches to her head and it was bound up, almost corpse-like, with a handkerchief. Marianne was frightened I think; and I was afraid Aunt Lumb, though not herself, and blind, (alas!) perceived it. The next time she begged to have a night-cap put on, and had a fig put behind her pillow, and MA was reconciled, and played about the room. She went in several times, and her coming always gave Aunt Lumb pleasure. It was such a beautiful Spring morning, that 1st of May, when Aunt Lumb died; such a contrast to the dreary weather before.

On the 3rd we all came back to Manchester; and then I rather began to fear that the long confinement in small rooms had told upon Marianne's temper, poor darling! She was fretful, and rather obstinate sometimes. But Betsy was leaving us, and a new servant coming, which I do think is a trial for a child. It soon wore off with patient, and gentle treatment from her Aunt Eliza, who was here at the time, comforting and being of use. We have never told her that Aunt Lumb was dead, fearing that a child's material ideas, might connect gloom with the idea of one so blessed. 'Gone to the rest prepared for the People of God!' But I often talk of her, and try to keep alive the recollection of her love and tenderness, and show her Aunt Lumb's picture, that even her bodily appearance (a fit shrine for so chastened and pure a spirit) may stand forth clear and distinct among her childhood remembrances.

One day we were talking, and she said 'Aunt Lumb was poorly'; 'No', I said, 'she is well and happy now'. Is she, replied my dear little girl, 'Oh then I am so glad; let me go and coax her'. And since she has been at Knutsford (in September) she has told me Aunt Lumb did not live with Aunt Ab now; she had left that house. I longed to say she was 'gone to a house not made with hands eternal, in the heavens'. But I thought I had better not, for to her it would have been unintelligible at present. Before she went to Knutsford in September she had again a few days of untract-ableness, and obstinacy. But I think she was very judiciously managed while there, for she came back a good little darling, so gentle and loving. Indeed I should say that her temper was very sweet, and her disposition very affectionate. Her little conscience too is becoming very acute and well-judging. I think most of the faults are of inadvertence (hardly *faults*;) except now and then when she has a fit of obstinacy; but we are very steady in fulfilling our *threat* of punishment, so these little obstinacies are gradually disappearing. Our punishment for her is taking her and leaving her alone for five minutes or so, in a *light* room. We tell her the length of time that she may not think we are influenced by caprice, or that she gains her point (of leaving the room) by crying. Once and once only have we had recourse to a severe punishment. It was one Sunday eveng it may be about five weeks ago; we were trying to teach her, her letters, more by way of occupation for her these long winter evenings, than from any anxiety as to her progress in learning. She knew all the vowels but refused to say A. All the others she would say, but would not even [?] repeat A after us. We got the slate, and drew it for her; but she persevered. Meta was asleep so we were unwilling to provoke the violent crying, which generally ensues when she is taken upstairs; so Wm gave her a slap on her hand every time she refused to say it, till at last she said it quite pat. Still I am sure we were so unhappy that we cried, when she was gone to bed. And I don't know if it was right. If not pray, dear Mari-anne, forgive us.

Since then we have not attempted any more lessons till she shows some desire to resume them; and I think she is coming round, for she delights in getting a book, and saying to herself, 'This is A' or O, as the case may be &c.

She is not by any means forward for her age; but not at all deficient in anything. She has never asked any question whatever that could lead to any, even the most simple truths, of religion. I am on the watch for anything of the sort.

She is getting both useful, and independent. She does little things for herself and other people, and thinks of things herself, such as fetching her Papa's slippers &c. Today he was going out; and she had gone on a message into the kitchen, but when she heard him trying to open the front door, she ran, calling out Stop Papa Papa; you must give me a kiss before you go.

And now for my little Meta; 10 months old on the fifth of this month. She has a much more passionate temper than Marianne; perhaps much livelier. But I sometimes fancy that 8 weeks spent day and night in one little close room, may have had some influence on her temper. She is very bright and saucy when all goes right, and very affectionate; particularly to her Papa and Elizabeth; little, saucy girl she prefers them both to her Mama. I fancy she will be more clever than her elder sister, if not so gentle. And there are very fine materials to work upon I am convinced, if I but know how. I am sometimes afraid Elizabeth spoils her. She has had very good health with the exception of one week, when she was about 9 months and a fortnight old; the same age and cutting the same teeth as MA was when she had her terrible illness. But if this was anything of the sort, it was not nearly so violent.

She has now had four teeth for 2 months or more. She is taller and slighter than MA and stronger, as she can roll and crawl away famously on the carpet. She is like MA; not quite such a pretty complexion, and no dimple, but longer eye-lashes. She can not quite stand by taking hold of anything, but very nearly. She has no little accomplishments yet, but that is only for want of being taught. She knows us all by name. Once or twice I have heard Elizabeth distracting her attention when in a little pet by telling her to look for Papa or Dicky (the bird) when they were not there. This I am afraid I did not sufficiently check.

The two dear little sisters are very fond of one another. Marianne gives up anything she has if Meta wants it. Almost too much I fancy sometimes. And Meta looks so relyingly for Marianne's help if she has lost any little plaything or in any distress. And she crows and dances when she hears Marianne's voice. Oh! how I hope this love will last. I must do my best to cherish it. Oh God help me in all my good resolutions with regard to these two dear children, for without them I have no strength. Amen.

March 25th 1838.[9] *Sunday Evening.*

There is a new era in the little life of my dear little girl. Tomorrow she goes to an Infant School. I think I am naturally undecided, or rather perhaps apt to repent my decision when it is too late, but now I am beginning to wonder if I have done right about this darling. There is much to be said on each side. It *may* weaken her pleasure in home, her love for us all, her confidence in me, at present such a blessing to me; – she *may* meet with children who may teach her the meaning of things of which at present we desire to keep her ignorant, that we may give her correct ideas when her mind is more advanced; such as Death, falsehood &c &c. But our reasons for wishing her to go to school, are also strong; not to advance her rapidly in any branch of learning, for William and I agree in not caring for this; but to perfect her habits of obedience, to give her an idea of conquering difficulties by perseverance; and to make her apply steadily for a short time. She is to go at half past nine, and come home at 12, and certainly not in the afternoon at present, if ever. I think enough of application may be got in the morning, and I shall like her to be with me, with Meta, out of doors &c &c, in the afternoon. I am sometimes afraid of becoming a lazy mother, willing to send my children away from me, and forgetting that on *me* lies the heaviest responsibility. I will try and be better in this respect. I intend as much as I can, to fetch her from school myself; I have several reasons for wishing to do this. One is that she may not be much out of school with the other children, though I have reason to believe them to be all respectable, and well brought up; but as she will be younger, she may the more easily catch up any false ideas. Then I mean to lead her to tell me in the course of her walk home, all the little events that have occurred in school. I can per-haps set her right if her ideas get confused, and I can sympathize with and advise her. I have tried to decide in this matter for the best, and now must await the result; only pray for God's blessing upon her.

Since I last wrote, she and I have begun to talk together about reli-gion. I have told her the simple truths I thought she could understand, such as God's goodness and love, His watching over us in the silent hours of the night &c. I think she has now right ideas as far as they go, about this important subject. At first she perplexed me very much by her very *material* questions. 'When does – go to bed', &c. But now we talk together in a low tone, and she likes to hear about him, and refers very properly to him as the 'Giver of every good thing'. (Not her words, of course.) Her Aunt Lizzy is coming here soon, and tonight I told her we should have Aunt Lizzy here in three weeks, if we were all well. 'But whom must we ask to keep us well'. (MA) 'God'. After a pause she added 'I shall ask God to keep Aunt Lizzy well too'. She went to chapel for the first and only time on Christmas day, & was I think a little tired, though she likes much to talk about it.

She has picked up all her large letters, and can arrange them so as to make Dog Cow, Horse. She can say 'the little Busy Bee' – but I do not know if she attaches much meaning to the words.

Her temper continues liable to the same fault obstinacy. In some moods if told to do a thing, she remains with her hand patting her mouth, almost like one stupid; it is then so difficult to move her, and it has been *most* difficult to find a judicious remedy. I am very sorry to say that after trying several, we have been obliged occasionally to give a slight whipping. It has been done sorrowfully and gently, and has never failed in making her more obedient, without producing the *least* resentful feeling. She is a sweet little creature in general; full of good feeling. She would give rather too freely to the poor. 'I love you, and Papa, & Meta, & Elizabeth, & Fanny, and poor people'. William says he fears I excite her sensibilities too much; I hope not, for I should dread it as much as he can do. I have no time to write about our dear little Meta tonight. I must devote my next '*chapter*' to her. In the mean time I may just mention that the two dear little sisters seem very fond of each other. May God bless them both, and preserve them to us. Nevertheless not my will be done, by [sic] thine O Lord. Amen.

April 8. Sunday Evening.

Just a fortnight ago since I wrote last, and since that time I have had a sad fright about Marianne, on last Friday but one she had an attack of croup about 8 o'clock in the evening. We heard a cough like a dog's bark. (She had had a cold in her head, and had seemed pale, and languid all day.) We gave her 24 drops of Ipec: wine, and Sam & Mr Partington both came. They said we had done quite rightly, and ordered her some calomel powders. Of course so much medicine, and the necessary confinement in the house have made her not so strong, and prevented her from going to school, but we have reason to be most thankful that she is spared to us, and I do earnestly and humbly hope that I am truly thankful. Poor little Eddy Deane was taken ill of croup on the same night, and died on the following Monday. (Oh! may I bring myself to a thorough resignation about the afflictions which God may see fit to send me; and Oh Lord, while I pray thee to preserve my darling children, may I not be too much wrapt up in them. Every proof of Marianne's delicacy seems to endear her more to me.[)]

When I last wrote in my Journal, I was stopped by the lateness of the hour before I had put down any particulars about Meta. I have been amused on looking at my former writing in this book to perceive the difference between the two little girls. Meta is far more independent than Marianne was at her age, which I suppose is owing to her having enjoyed more uninterrupted good health. She can crawl about anywhere as quickly as many children walk, and if the door is open, she is in the passage directly making towards the kitchen. She even raises herself by anything on to her feet, but has no idea of walking. She will play on the floor for an hour at a time in preference to being nursed. She has no idea of talking, though she is constantly singing and making noises. She is very affectionate, but not so sensitive as MA was, for instance she does not in the least care for being laughed at, but rather enjoys a joke. But I am afraid she runs some little danger of being spoilt, for nearly every one in the house pets her, and she is very full of caprices, and sometimes gives way to sad little fits of passion, if she is a little bit affronted by the most trifling thing. I am sometimes afraid she is not checked enough; Elizabeth (her nurse) always says 'poor thing, it is time enough to begin' – This I know is wrong, though I am not sure if I act upon my knowledge. Meta loves her Papa so warmly that I think his influence may do much towards conquering her little passions. If he says 'naughty little Meta' she sobs as if her heart would break, so of course we avoid such a working upon her sensibility. She is generous in giving a piece of anything she likes, but not good in giving up a plaything, and whenever she sees Marianne occupied or amused by anything, that is the very thing she wants to have. She wants every eatable or drinkable she sees others having, and what is more likes them all down to rhubarb and magnesia.

In general the sisters are very kind to one another, though sometimes I have been sorry to see Marianne, without any anger, or any apparent bad feeling, hurt little Meta, knowing that she hurts her. I think it must be from the love of power, but of course we try to check it. May God bless & *preserve* them both –

October 14 (38) Sunday Evening.
My dear little girls are both pretty well and healthy. How thankful I ought to be; and I do feel thankful for the blessings, I have in my children. I hope they are improving in every way. Marianne has begun since her birthday (Sep 12) to read and sew, and makes pretty good progress, especially in the working time. I am glad of something that will occupy her, for I have some difficulty in finding her occupation, and she does not *set herself* to any employment. In this respect I think Meta will be very different. She is almost always busy – sometimes in mischief to be sure, but she is much the most energetic of the two sisters. I wish very much to make Marianne industrious; I am afraid I do not set her a good example. I try to employ her in making candlelighters, pricking pictures, counting out articles &c, but she is soon tired of any *one* employment. This must be struggled against for I can tell from experience how increasing an error this is. In temper and habits of obedience I think MA is much improved. She has much less frequently those fits of obstinacy she used to have. I am so happy to see her (general) desire of doing right, and I try to exercise her conscience by occasionally leaving her to judge if such an action be right or not. She is very affectionate, and this again is a circumstance to be thankful[10] for. She has not yet overcome her excitability, and we find it necessary to keep[11] her very quiet, as otherwise she suffers much from exhaustion which shows itself in increased irritability.

Oct. 28. Sunday Evening.

I was interrupted when I last wrote, but I shall try and make up for it tonight. Marianne and I are going in a[12] day to Prospect Hill, on account of her health; she has grown very much lately, and her Uncle Sam thinks it desirable for her to have a little change of air before winter sets in. I hope it will do her good, but there are so many things in another person's house that one cannot regulate (meals, temperature &c) that I feel a little anxious. I think I did not mention in my last account that since she was four years old (Sep 12) she has begun to have regular little lessons; before that time indeed she had learnt her letters, partly in play. – She began with one word a day, in 'Mama's lessons', but as of course it was one *new* word, she now sometimes reads nearly a line. She seems to like it and takes pains. Sometimes in her sewing lessons (of six stitches in seaming), I fear I am not patient enough. Oh God, in whose hands are all hearts make me more even-tempered. With her I do try a great deal, but Oh my Father help me to regulate my impatient temper better!

She is a most sympathetic little thing. She tries so to comfort me if she sees me looking sad, or thinks that anything has happened to discompose me. Her great faults are[13] unaccountable fits of obstinacy; which are I hope diminishing and a want of perseverance and dependance [sic] upon others as to her occupations and amusements. I have begun to teach her a little prayer morning and night, merely a few words, of thanksgiving and blessing. I am not sure that she attaches much devotional feeling to this observance, but I thought it desirable to lead her to something beyond the visible and material, and some day I hope more interest will be shown as to the Being to whom they are addressed. She also comes in every morning, while her Papa reads from Doddridge's Expositor and prays. I sometimes fear this service is too long for her, but I think she likes coming in, though at first we had a great struggle, owing I think to a sort of nervous shyness. God bless and preserve my darling Marianne!

As to dear little Meta, she is totally different from Marianne though very like her in person. She is a more popular character: very lively, enjoying a joke, always busy for herself; but she is passionate and wilful, though less so I think than she was. She is a most generous little creature, always ready to give away eatables. Not *so* generous as to her playthings, but often very good about that. She has many engaging ways kissing if she thinks she has offended or hurt in any way. She is very backward in her talking, – Tata being the only word she can say – with an attempt at 'please'. But she understands and notices every word that is spoken before her, and makes herself understood too by signs and noises. She has walked this two months, being a very good walker at 18 months. She has just cut her last eye-tooth, and I am glad that trial is over for her, poor darling, though she has not suffered much to what many children do, Marianne has within this fortnight begun to have a little animal food, but we keep Meta to the old plain diet. May God bless both my dear children.

Notes

1. Verso blank at this point.
2. Inserted word.
3. Altered from 'I'.
4. Deleted letters.
5. Inserted word.
6. Altered word.
7. Inserted word.
8. Inserted word.
9. '8' altered from '7'.
10. Altered word.
11. Altered from 'for her to be kept'.
12. Inserted word.
13. Altered word.

Sophia Holland's Diary

Critical introduction

Anita Wilson

A diary kept by Marianne's future mother-in-law, Sophia Isaac Holland, provides an additional view of Gaskell family history and of Victorian social history. In 1832, the same year as Elizabeth and William Gaskell's marriage, Sophia married Edward Holland, who was Mrs Gaskell's first cousin. Edward was a member of Parliament and served as an executor of Hannah Lumb's will after her death in 1837. He also made some investments on behalf of the Gaskells; in a gracious letter dated 13 January 1849, Mrs Gaskell thanked him for his 'very kind & advantageous' advice (*Letters*, no. 39a, p. 827). She and her children often visited the Hollands at their country estate, Dumbleton Hall, in Gloucestershire.

Edward Holland was also Charles Darwin's second cousin, and the Darwin family correspondence provides an interesting range of opinions regarding Edward's bride. On the Hollands' wedding day, Charles's sister Catherine reported the disdainful reaction of their brother Erasmus to the new Mrs Holland: 'vulgar and sulky,' she 'is not only stupid herself, but makes other people stupid …' (to Charles Darwin, 26 April 1832, qtd. in Burkhardt and Smith, p. 229). After visiting the Hollands five months later, Catherine endorsed Erasmus's dislike of Sophia, whom she described as 'a disagreeable, little, dull, cold thing' (to Charles Darwin, 14 October 1832, *ibid.*, p. 275). Edward, who had begun building Dumbleton Hall, was dismissed as 'awfully pompous'; Miss Darwin was clearly not impressed by 'the grand ceremony of laying the first stone –' (to Charles Darwin, 14 October 1832, *ibid.*, p. 275).

When the Edward Hollands visited the elder Mr Darwin during their wedding tour, Charles's sister Susan was pleasantly surprised to find Sophia 'rather pretty & a nice little creature all together & particularly well suited to Edward who seemed very proud of her' (to Charles Darwin, 12 May 1832, *ibid.*, p. 235). Although the 'little M^rs. H. [was] very shy', Susan apparently sympathized with the nineteen-year-old bride. The diminutive language suggests both affection and condescension while emphasizing Sophia's child-like and vulnerable qualities.

This branch of the Holland family was more affluent than the middle-class Gaskells and was larger, with three sons and six daughters. Edward Thurstan, who would marry Marianne Gaskell in 1866, was the Hollands' second child, their first son, and the central figure in a diary which his mother kept from his birth in February 1836 until July 1839. Thurstan's physical, intellectual, and spiritual growth was recorded, along with an analysis of his evolving personality and of his relationships with parents, nurse, and siblings. Although Gaskell's diary is of greater literary quality, both works show respect for children's individuality and a remarkable degree of insight regarding child development. Like Gaskell, Holland reveals that Victorian mothers were astute psychologists long before psychology became a household word.

Both mothers observed their infants closely and were fascinated by early signs of emergent personalities. In six months of motherhood, Gaskell was surprised to discover that even very young babies were interesting people. Her first entry opens with regret that she had not begun the diary sooner, 'for (though I should have laughed at the idea twelve months ago) there have been many little indications of disposition &c. already; which I can not now remember clearly' (Gaskell diary, p. 50).

Holland had a head start on her journal which Gaskell might have envied; the first entry summarized Thurstan's first eight weeks. Reading between the lines, one can glimpse Holland's pleasure in her precise account of Thurstan's first smile ('between 3 and 4 weeks old – 2d smile a week after –') and her relief when his crying fits diminished (p. 89).[1] In contrast to Gaskell, however, Holland gave very little explicit discussion of her own emotions as she recorded her child's behaviour. Winifred Gérin's description of Gaskell's diary as 'a little mine of observation, penetration, and perception that is as revealing of the mother as of the child observed' (Gérin, p. 54) would not apply to the Holland diary.

When writing about the affective bond which developed between mother and baby, Holland adopted a rather detached tone. At five months, she noted, Thurstan began 'to hold out his arms to come to me to be fed –' (p. 89). A month later, he cried to come to his mother when he was not hungry, showing that his attachment extended beyond the need for food. At eleven months, he immediately obeyed his mother when she told him to return a toy to his sister. Before Thurstan's first birthday, his mother had become a source of emotional nurturance as well as a figure of authority, but the reader can only guess at how Holland may have felt about these developments. Gaskell's frequent expressions of delight, pride, and anxiety are notably absent.

This difference in tone, which with a few exceptions extends throughout Holland's diary, may reflect the context of each woman's motherhood. Gaskell had experienced a stillbirth and had never known her own mother; her diary became an outlet for intense love, longing, and fear of loss. Holland's diary gives the impression that she was more secure and less thrilled about motherhood. She already had a healthy daughter when Thurstan was born, and a second son was born during the period covered in the diary. Holland may simply have been too busy to write in a more contemplative fashion about child-rearing. Gaskell's diary served as a psychological insurance policy against the child's loss of her mother or the mother's loss of her child. It is not clear what motivated Holland to keep a diary; did she begin after the birth of her second child because she wished to record her eldest son's early years for posterity? Or was the diary the equivalent of a private photo album for maternal reminiscences? Her entries have the quality of sharply focused snapshots, which capture moments in a child's life but rarely give a glimpse of the photographer.

Despite their stylistic differences, the two diaries share much common ground regarding child-rearing and discipline. Both mothers sought to apply patience and reason rather than slaps and whippings. Except for one reference to the Edgeworths, Holland does not mention any child-rearing literature, but her kindly and judicious approach to discipline is consistent with the advice of contemporary authorities. The only mention of corporal punishment in the Holland diary occurs in the penultimate entry, when three-year-old Thurstan refused to take a nap. Sophia's patience was running out, and after repeated admonitions she warned Thurstan that he would be punished if he did not settle down in two minutes. '"Are you go[ing] to whip me"?' Thurstan inquired. '"What shall you whip me with"?' (p. 100).

The mother's response provides a reassuring anticlimax to the little drama: 'I told him I should have his nightgown put on –' (p. 100). Apparently Thurstan was aware of whippings, but he seems more intrigued than fearful. His behaviour was hardly that of a child oppressed by harsh discipline. When he continued to defy orders by bouncing in bed and 'peepg thro the curtains', he was not allowed to go downstairs for dinner. Like Marianne Gaskell, who confounded her parents by making a game of standing in the corner, Thurstan turned punishment into pleasure by enjoying his allotted slice of bread in bed. His mother clearly did not want him to go hungry, nor did she turn the episode into a do-or-die battle of wills; Thurstan 'had got into so restless a state that I felt it better to let him go down without further punishment', she concluded (p. 100).

In comparison to Gaskell, Holland appears more confident and less agonized about discipline, probably because she possessed more experience as a parent. If Holland ever felt, as Gaskell did, '... oh! so cast down by [a child's] wrong-doing' (Gaskell diary, p. 61), she did not write about such feelings. Nothing in Holland's diary is comparable to the painful confrontation over Marianne's ABCs and the Gaskells' subsequent remorse. The first recorded 'quarrel', in Holland's words, between mother and son took place when Thurstan was fourteen months old and wanted to climb on a tub in his mother's room. "Cryed passionately when I took him away & crawled there again', she reported (p. 92). Thurstan was removed but not punished. About two weeks later, he tried a more devious strategy, admiring the flowers on the forbidden tub while gradually maneuvering to climb it. 'Saw first instance of slyness', Holland noted, but she did not seem perturbed by this development (p. 92).

Thurstan's bouts of naughtiness were taken in stride. At seventeen months, he knocked over the nursery breakfast table and 'shewed every sign of delight at the mischief he had occasioned, laughing and jumping about' (p. 93). It must have been quite a scene, but Holland did not mention any punishment. Instead, she calmly observed that Thurstan was 'Very fond of climbing a stool, chair, the steps by my bed or any thing he can reach' (p. 94). Thurstan was more energetic than Marianne, and his rambunctious behaviour seems to have been accepted as part of his toddler phase. Gender roles undoubtedly influenced Holland's perception of her son's activity, which was far removed from the feminine quietness that Gaskell cherished in Marianne. After describing the overturned table, Holland discussed Thurstan's tussles with his older sister, which he initiated by pushing her. 'According to present appearances he will soon be the Master', Holland concluded matter-of-factly (p. 94).

A year and a half later, allowances continued to be made for childish exuberance. Obedience was not optional, but a child was not expected to act like a miniature adult. When Thurstan became too boisterous, his mother offered a sensible compromise – he could run about and make all the noise he liked in another room, then return when he felt calmer. '"Yes me is a little bit naughty"', three-year-old Thurstan agreed, and his mother's prescription worked with no hard feelings on either side (p. 96). After releasing some energy and 'makg good use of his lungs', Holland reported, Thurstan 'knocked at the door & told me he was good –' (p. 96).

Immediately after describing this ideal scenario of co-operation between parent and child, Holland discussed early language acquisition. Thurstan and his sister were trying to imitate adult speech, with mixed success, but they could be understood with little difficulty: 'Teddy [Thurstan] told me "I *drinkted* some water" & Missie talks of the things GMamma *gaven* her' (p. 96). The juxtaposition of topics suggests that Holland enlisted Thurstan's rudimentary grasp of language to defuse conflicts and to encourage him to 'talk about the consequences of [his] conduct', as Gaskell said of Marianne.

A month later, Holland discovered Thurstan and his cousin, Swinton:

> breaking the animals of the Noah's Ark, checked them at first but remembering Edgeworth's opinion of playthings I said if you wish to break any more you must bring them to me & ask leave to do so. Thurstan brought some, I consented & heard Swin say 'Now we will kill this one' & talking of breakg their legs. (p. 97)

The Noah's Ark was one of the most popular Victorian nursery toys, combining fun with a higher purpose, zoological or theological. Thurstan's gleeful destruction was obviously not the sort of play his mother had in mind, and her initial impulse was to put a stop to it. Instead, she required the miscreants to follow a rather formal procedure of receiving licence to be naughty, which was probably an attempt to diminish a forbidden thrill by making it legal. This is the only episode in Holland's diary which refers to a child-care book, probably *Practical Education* (1798), by Richard Edgeworth and his daughter Maria.[2]

The Edgeworths advocated a hands-on approach to learning (perhaps Thurstan and Swinton took this a bit too literally) and favoured simple toys which encouraged children to learn through experience – blocks of various shapes and sizes for babies, a 'rational toyshop' filled with puzzles, arts and crafts, tools, and gardening equipment for older children, even a child-sized printing press. Toy furniture was designed to be taken apart and reassembled by small hands, not to repose in the regal splendour of a doll's house. Parents remained in charge, but they worked with, rather than against, the natural tendencies of early childhood – energy, inquisitiveness, short attention spans, the desire to manipulate and experiment with playthings. Thurstan was entitled to break his toys if he wished, provided that he received permission to do so.

The Edgeworths' sensible and humane approach to discipline was compatible with the progressive Unitarian philosophy, which rejected the idea that children were vessels of original sin whose wills must be broken. A family connection existed as well. Until the age of eleven, Elizabeth Gaskell was taught at home by her aunts. It is probable that Hannah Lumb and her younger unmarried sister, Abigail Holland, 'favoured a child-oriented teaching, like that advised by Maria Edgeworth and her father Richard in their *Practical Education* ...' (Uglow, p. 27). Maria Edgeworth was also a friend and correspondent of Mary Holland, who was cousin both to Elizabeth Gaskell and Edward Holland. Mary's father, Dr Peter Holland, probably inspired the character of Mr Gibson, the country doctor in Gaskell's *Wives and Daughters*. In 1874, Mary's niece visited Knutsford and remarked upon the collection of old letters: '... Edgeworth's, Barbauld's, Aitken's [sic], Darwin's, Wedgewood's [sic], all that old set. Sir Henry Holland always figures as the fashionable young man in the vortex of London society. Miss Edgeworth's letters are charming, and there are drawers full of them.'[3]

This breezy catalogue of 'that old set' from a younger generation's perspective reveals the web of personal and professional connections among prominent Unitarian families. Maria Edgeworth had met Dr Holland's oldest son, Henry, in Ireland in 1809. A suave character and a man rising rapidly in the world, Henry was eventually appointed physician to Queen Victoria and was knighted in 1857. Gaskell had read Anna Laetitia Barbauld's *Lessons for Children* (1778–9) and *Hymns in Prose for Children* (1781). Barbauld (1743–1825) sought to inspire young children with a reverent awareness of the divine presence in the natural world, 'by connecting religion with a variety of sensible objects'.[4] Since Barbauld's *Hymns* remained popular during the Victorian era, it is quite possible that Elizabeth Gaskell and Sophia Holland used this book in teaching their own children.

Edgeworth and her father admired Barbauld's work, although they avoided the topic of religion in their own books out of distaste for sectarian controversy. Maria Edgeworth is remembered for her didactic yet sprightly tales which conveyed messages without sacrificing either her characters' individuality or her young readers' patience. In her best known story, 'The Purple Jar' (1796; rpt. 1801), the little girl Rosamond needs new shoes but longs for an eye-catching purple jar in a shop window.[5] Rosamond's mother, à la Rousseau, allows her daughter to choose and, of course, Rosamond selects what she desires at the moment rather than what she needs. The alluring jar turns out to be filled with smelly dye, and Rosamond misses an excursion because her shoes have worn out.[6] Rosamond's mother could afford to purchase the shoes as well as the jar; rationality, not money, is the issue. Edgeworth implies that a girl must learn to think rather than act upon impulse, especially in the context of a consumer society and its manipulative strategies. But she makes her point, while also making Rosamond a credible and appealing character. Even after her débâcle, Rosamond is never a moralistic paper doll. She tells her mother, '... I am sure – no not quite sure – but I hope I shall be wiser another time' (qtd. in Demers and Moyles, p. 145).

Sophia Holland and Elizabeth Gaskell had probably read Edgeworth's stories as children; did a trace of Rosamond's humanity lodge in Gaskell's consciousness when she created characters like Mary Barton and Ruth?[7] 'I am glad you like Mary', Gaskell told Tottie Fox, 'I do: but people are angry with her just because she is not perfect' (Letters, no. 48, p. 82). And Edgeworth's didacticism was more liberating than it may appear at first glance; she treated girls as reasonable people who make decisions and who have brains as well as feelings – very similar to Gaskell's aspirations for Marianne.[8]

March 1839 must have been a lively month in the Holland household. Shortly after the Noah's Ark demolition, Thurstan's mother found him stirring the fire with a poker while his sister watched with pleasure. After making the children sit apart for a time, Holland 'told them a story of a child being burnt' (p. 98). This is the only occasion recorded in Holland's diary when she deliberately tried to scare the children into obedience, no doubt because their mischief had been potentially dangerous. Even enlightened Unitarian mothers sometimes had to resort to old-fashioned threats. There was no shortage of sources for such grisly stories, which had been a staple of eighteenth- and early nineteenth-century children's literature. These cautionary tales reappeared as parodies in Lewis Carroll's Alice in Wonderland:

> ... [Alice] had read several nice little stories about children who had got burnt, and eaten up by wild beasts, and other unpleasant things, all because they would not remember the simple rules their friends had taught them: such as, that a red-hot poker will burn you if you hold it too long ... and she had never forgotten that, if you drink much from a bottle marked 'poison,' it is almost certain to disagree with you, sooner or later. (Ch. 1)

The collusion of 'Missie' Holland in her brother's mischief is one manifestation of a sibling relationship whose mingled affection and rivalry is charted throughout Sophia Holland's diary. Unlike Marianne Gaskell, Thurstan was never an only child. The diary's second entry, written when Thurstan was three months old, connects his dawning powers of observation with his sister's proximity: 'First began to notice things in the park passing before him – Likes to look at his Sister; – smiling as he watches her –' (p. 89). At eight months, Thurstan's interest in Missie was not so benign: 'Fond of pulling his Sisters hair – gives a cunning look as he does it & watches to hear if she cries out' (p. 90). Among Thurstan's first words were 'go away', directed to his sister. At fourteen months, he showed a sense of revenge for the first time by refusing to kiss his sister when she had been unkind to him. Later that month, the shoe was on the other foot; Thurstan was 'a most loving admiring Brother. Tho Missy [sic] still cannot get over a jealous feeling towards him' (p. 92).

As Thurstan grew beyond babyhood, Holland continued to observe the interesting little nuances and paradoxes of his feelings toward Missie. He imitated his sister at the table – 'This is not the case when with me at dinner', Holland noted with perhaps a touch of wry humour (p. 94) – was generous about sharing food and toys, but turned down a treat 'because he thought his piece not so large as his Sister's' (p. 94). While vigilant about getting his fair share of goodies, Thurstan was also protective of his sister. At age three, he took on the traditional masculine role of defender. When younger brother Fred (making one of his rare appearances in the diary) shoved Missie and hurt her slightly, he promptly received 'a strong push which sent him to the floor' from Thurstan. Holland settled the squabble impartially, but, in a rare statement of her own feelings, she privately expressed satisfaction with Thurstan's chivalrous behaviour: '– I like this spirit of Thurstan for he does not defend himself' (p. 98). In the next entry, life was back to normal, and Missie's champion was standing in the nursery corner because he had teased her.

Holland recorded these ups and downs of sibling devotion and rivalry with apparent equanimity. Gaskell expressed pleasure and concern more overtly when writing about Marianne and Meta. Her keen sense of responsibility for nurturing their relationship emerges strongly. 'Oh! how I hope this love [between the sisters] will last. I must do my best to cherish it', she vowed (Gaskell diary, p. 66). Because of her own family history, Gaskell did not take sibling relationships for granted. She treasured every sign of affection between her daughters and showed some pain in recounting their inevitable conflicts: 'In general the sisters are very kind to one another, though sometimes I have been sorry to see Marianne, without any anger, or any apparent bad feeling, hurt little Meta, knowing that she hurts her' (Gaskell diary, p. 69).

Both women attribute such conflicts to the 'love of power', a phrase which appears in both diaries, but Holland seems to have been less perturbed by the perpetual outbursts among her children. Here and elsewhere in the two diaries, it is impossible to ascertain whether a difference in style may be indicative of a difference in attitude. With six children yet to come, however, one would hope that Sophia Holland did indeed possess the equable temperament projected in her writing. The last sentence of her diary does not presage a tranquil future: '[Thurstan was] Very naughty for some day[s] squeaking if Missie or Fred touched his playthings & often teazg them' (p. 100).

Thurstan's father is largely invisible amidst these domestic dramas. The Holland diary includes no episodes in which the parents collaborate in disciplining a child, discuss child-rearing, or share their misgivings, as the Gaskells did. Of course, the fact that such incidents are not recorded does not mean that they did not occur, but the omission may indicate that Sophia Holland perceived the father's parental role as secondary to a greater extent than Elizabeth Gaskell did.

The few glimpses of Edward Holland suggest that he and his children enjoyed each other's company. At fifteen months, Thurstan was 'Very much disappointed to find that Papa was not rolled up in the bed curtains this morning, where he often has hidden himself when the children come in' (p. 93). Thurstan and Marianne both learned to say 'Papa' as one of their first words, 'leaving poor *Mama* in the back ground', as Gaskell put it (Gaskell diary, p. 58). Holland likewise observed that Thurstan was 'Very fond of Papa – Constantly calls for him. – He seldom calls Mamma tho when with me he does not always like going away' (p. 93).[9] For the most part, however, Gaskell's account shows a stronger bond between father and children. At fourteen months, Meta was so fond of her father that both parents took care not to exploit this attachment. Even a mild paternal rebuke reduced the ebullient Meta to tears; 'so of course we avoid such a working upon her sensibility', Mrs Gaskell firmly concluded (Gaskell diary, p. 69). In the pages of his wife's diary, at any rate, Edward Holland was not such a presence in his children's lives.

In both families, early education was the mother's province. Thurstan started young, even by Victorian standards. The Edgeworths recommended that lessons in reading commence at age four. At two and a half, Thurstan began learning a few letters each day. As he progressed, he called himself 'a schoolboy' (p. 95). His mother's lessons were informal, even playful; they began 'by imitating the cries of animals picking out a few from Noah's Ark' (p. 95). This approach follows the Edgeworths' philosophy, that '[b]y kind patience, and well timed, distinct, and above all, by short lessons, a young child may be initiated in the mysteries of learning, and in the first principles of knowledge, without fatigue, or punishment, or tears' (qtd. in Uglow, p. 27).[10]

No tearful scenes over reading lessons appear in Holland's diary. But her expectations were high, since she had successfully taught Thurstan's older sister. At two years and eight months, Thurstan enjoyed his lessons but was not progressing to his mother's satisfaction. He 'has not any thing like the memory of Missie', Holland noted with some consternation.'Round O and Crooked S are the only two letters I can feel sure he will know – The differences of form wh Missie when once they were pointed out to her never forgot, seem to make little impression on him –' (p. 95).

Even those two letters are quite an achievement for a toddler who only recently had 'left off sucking his fingers …' (p. 95). Holland's brief narrative has an uncharacteristic tone of anxiety; would Thurstan ever learn the alphabet? Her worry is exaggerated, but understandable given the manifold pressures upon Victorian mothers to raise ideal children. Sophia must have been relieved when, on his third birthday, Thurstan knew 'nearly all his large letters & a few of the small & tho sometimes rather inattentive likes saying his lesson very much' (p. 96).

Along with his reading lessons, Thurstan received the rudiments of religious education from his mother. Gaskell worried because Marianne had displayed no interest in religion by the age of three; at two and a half, Thurstan often asked to kneel and pray with his mother, who would give him a few simple words which he repeated with appropriate solemnity. Whatever understanding he may have possessed at this age, the ritual of prayer was important to him, perhaps as a source of security. One night he awakened late and 'would not be happy without saying his prayers' to his mother (p. 96).

Like Elizabeth Gaskell, Sophia Holland talked with her children about religion in a reverent yet informal fashion. She was neither condescending nor intimidating. Her very young acolytes, free to voice their own concerns, posed some tough questions. 'God loves us even when we are naughty, but not so much as when we are good', Holland counselled. Regrettably, she did not record her response to Missie's follow-up question: '"Does God love us when we are a little bit naughty Mamma?"' (p. 98).

Thurstan, aged three years and two months at the time, had already engaged in some remarkably sophisticated dialogues with his mother.'"Will our bodies go to heaven when we die"?', he inquired. Holland 'tried to make him understand a difference between body & soul & told him that Jesus Christ would come again & would then take our bodies to heaven –' (p. 99): a challenging concept for a three-year-old, to say the least. But Holland was following Thurstan's lead, not pressuring him, and he grasped the essential point very well. Three months later, Holland explained how a butterfly dies after laying its eggs. Blending natural history and theology, Thurstan asked, '"Does Jesus Christ come to take their bodies to Heaven?"' (p. 99).

Hell is not mentioned in Holland's diary, and religion has no threatening connotations. The closest she comes to acknowledging the possibility of damnation is a gently phrased admonition that 'if we do not try to be good' we will not go to Heaven (p. 98). As in the Gaskell household, the spiritual education of children focused upon divine love, protection, and forgiveness.[11] This constructive and psychologically healthy approach contrasts sharply with the upbringing of Mary Haldane, a Methodist, who was about ten years older than Thurstan and Marianne. The religious anxiety which shadowed her childhood was not unusual in Victorian households, whether of 'Church' or 'Chapel' persuasion:

> I used to have passages of the Bible to learn, or poetry, if I misbehaved … I was often kept awake by thought of the sinfulness of my nature and with the sense that at any moment judgement might be passed upon me. I knew and felt that I was a great sinner and that God was my judge and must condemn me. I used to try to keep the Commandments of God, which I learned by heart, but constantly failed, and I was miserable … (qtd. in Pollock, pp. 220–1.)[12]

Thurstan's religious sensibility was not morbid, nor did his mother portray him as a spiritual paragon. The passage in Holland's diary which precedes Thurstan's meditation upon butterflies and resurrection includes the homely detail that spitting was 'a favourite entertainment of the young gentleman's …' (p. 99). But Thurstan showed considerably more interest in religion than Marianne did at the same age, despite a similar upbringing. His lively imagination may have stimulated his interest in religious topics and caused him to feel more acutely the need for divine love and protection.

Holland remarked upon Thurstan's 'strength of imagination' (p. 97) – not a phrase which Gaskell would have used to describe Marianne, who even at the age of three was more practical than fanciful. Sometimes Thurstan scared himself with his own fantasies; he was convinced that lions lived under the sofa and worried that they might turn up elsewhere. At three years and four months, he asked his mother, '"Will God keep us safe from the lions"? "When we are walking out of doors"?' Her rational explanation that 'there were no lions living in this country' failed to satisfy Thurstan, who replied, '"But I do pretend there are lions"'. Holland evidently settled the matter by offering spiritual reassurance along with a geography lesson: 'I talked to him for some time of the care of God & of the country where the lions live' (p. 99).

Thurstan was not always so serious; he made his mother laugh when he thought that an overturned basket resembled an elephant, and he pretended that the dinner glasses were a family – 'Papa', 'Mamma', and 'their little Sammy' (p. 97). But his readiness to look beyond literal and practical dimensions of experience may well have fuelled his fascination with the realm of religion and 'things invisible to see'.

An unspecified illness may also have contributed to Thurstan's vulnerability and occasioned the most tender and reflective passage in his mother's diary:

> Our dear boy has never yet recovered his illness – Probably he never will again possess that daring courage which he showed before. His nerves have been weakened and tho' his *moral courage* is not in the least

diminished, he has not the same amount of physical courage. I see this when he is with other children & often I perceive it in an increased sensibility greater than a child of his age should possess. – And which if encouraged may become a source of misery to him thro' life. – I never I believe should appeal to his affections in askg any thing. (p. 100)

Holland generally wrote with a more casual sense of affection. Nowhere else in the diary did she describe Thurstan (or the other children) as 'dear', nor did she express anxiety about their health, apart from passing references to teething and other routine ailments. Like Jane Austen, Holland used 'sensibility' to refer to emotional responsiveness, a quality which could be appealing in a child but also alarming in excess. Her resolution not to manipulate Thurstan's affections is similar to the Gaskells' care not to capitalize upon Meta's fondness for her father. The charm of affective precociousness had to be resisted for the child's benefit. When Marianne was only a year old, Gaskell was surprised to see her weeping over 'unexpected pleasure' and worried about 'managing these sensibilities, so beautiful when healthy, & so distressing when morbid' (Gaskell diary, p. 56). Both mothers believed that emotions too highly attuned were a potential source of future unhappiness as the child matured. A few years later, Marianne's sentimental proclamations of affection for family, servants and the poor were not altogether welcomed by either of her parents: 'William says he fears I excite her sensibilities too much; I hope not, for I should dread it as much as he can do' (Gaskell diary, p. 68). Marianne was certainly brought up with a social conscience and consciousness, but emotional gushing was frowned upon.

Distrust of excessive 'sensibility' reflected the Unitarian predilection for reason and distaste for emotional exhibitions of religious fervour. It was also consistent with much of eighteenth- and early nineteenth-century children's literature, including that of Maria Edgeworth. Holland and Gaskell were rooted in a rational conception of childhood, which neither denigrated nor deified the role of emotions. As they were writing their diaries, a new image of childhood was beginning to dominate both Victorian children's literature and portrayals of children in adult novels. Delicate, exquisitely (or unbearably) sensitive juvenile characters professed their love for God and for the poor, which frequently culminated in a tear-jerking deathbed scene. Encouraged by Evangelicalism and by Dickensian pathos, this sentimental trend had not quite taken hold in the 1830s. Ironically, the very traits which worried Holland and Gaskell would soon become fashionable, as the 'Cult of Sensibility' and the 'Romantic Child' held sway.[13]

Holland's account of Thurstan's early childhood ends with an enigmatic fragment, '– Noah's Ark –' (p. 100). Were more toy animals dismembered, or would Sophia have written about an entirely different incident? She presumably jotted down this phrase to jog her memory, then never resumed the diary due to pressures of time and a growing family. Each diary ends –

or stops – in a fashion which suits the writer's style. Holland typically seems to be writing in haste; her entries are filled with dashes and rush from one topic to another, rather like Gaskell's letters in later years. More coherent and reflective, Gaskell's diary also conveys more anxiety about motherhood and child-rearing. Her last entry concludes with a prayer, one of many throughout the diary: 'May God bless both my dear children' (Gaskell diary, p. 71).

In her own way, each woman has left a valuable legacy. Victorian mothers have too often been sentimentalized as domestic icons or deconstructed as victims of a repressive era. By preserving the texture of their daily lives, rough edges and all, Elizabeth Gaskell and Sophia Holland invite us to respect that elusive figure, the Victorian mother, as an individual in her own right, and to hear her voice.

Notes

1. Page references to quotations from Holland's diary apply to this new edition; all punctuation and spelling have been reproduced.
2. See *Practical Education*, vol. I, where the Edgeworths advise that a child breaks toys 'not from the love of mischief, but from the hatred of idleness; either he wishes to see what his playthings are made of, and how they are made; or, whether he can put them together again, if the parts be once separated. All this is perfectly innocent ...' (p. I).
3. A. W. Ward, Knutsford Edition, vol. 2, *Cranford and Other Tales*, p. xxi, quotes from *Letters of Mary Sibylla Holland*, ed. Bernard Holland, 1898.
4. Qtd. in Bator, p. 116. This reprinted edition, originally published in 1880 by John Murray, affirms the longevity of Barbauld's work (Bator, p. 115).
5. 'The Purple Jar' was first published in *The Parent's Assistant*, by Maria Edgeworth, with a preface by Richard Edgeworth (1796) and was reprinted in *Early Lessons* (1801). The 1796 edition received a favourable notice from Mary Wollstonecraft in the *Analytical Review* (Myers, 'Impeccable Governesses', p. 36).
6. Jackson (Ch. 7) discusses the modifications of Rousseau's educational theories in Edgeworth's work. Her oldest brother had been raised according to Rousseau's philosophy, with unfortunate results; the new Émile was a 'peevish, gauche, unsteady' young man (p. 152; see also Coveney, p. 47). Like Rousseau, Maria Edgeworth emphasized learning from experience as a key to moral education. However, her stories challenged Rousseau's romanticizing of emotion and also gave prominence to female characters. *Émile* was largely a masculine domain; his female counterpart had a far more restrictive upbringing as preparation for her sole purpose in life – to become Émile's wife.
7. Gaskell did not think highly of her limited ventures into children's literature. She wrote two rather preachy stories for the *Sunday School Penny Magazine*: 'Hand and Heart' (1849) and 'Bessy's Troubles at Home' (1852). Although Gaskell was inspired by the magazine's Unitarian founder, Travers Madge, to become more active in the Sunday school movement, she dismissed her literary contributions in a letter to Marianne: 'The children who like Bessy's Troubles are

great geese, & no judges at all, which children generally are, for it is complete rubbish I am sorry to say' (*Letters*, no. 114a, p. 845).

8.   Maria Edgeworth is a major figure in a tradition of children's literature written by women who resisted social and literary constructs of femininity as emotional, weak, and unintellectual. See Sarah Fielding, *The Governess, or, Little Female Academy* (1749) and Mary Wollstonecraft, whose *Original Stories from Real Life* (1788) preceded her touchstone of feminist literature, *A Vindication of the Rights of Woman* (1792). The Romantic movement's privileging of imagination and emotion created an enduring negative bias against these female authors, who were 'repudiating the old associations of the feminine with the irrational, and aspiring to be recognized as reasonable beings who might be permitted to join the closed circle of male discourse' (Briggs, p. 233; see also Myers). Darton (Ch. IX) provides an overview of Edgeworth's contributions to children's literature.

9.   Ironically, the mother may be less present in her child's early language because she is such a constant and immediate presence in the child's daily life; the absent father must be recalled or summoned through language: '... in a system of representation, the figure requires the absence of the referent' (Homans, p. 169).

10.   See *Practical Education*, vol. II, p. 286. The Edgeworths also state in this passage that they consider attention 'as the faculty of the mind which is essential to the cultivation of all its other powers'. Gaskell may have been influenced by this view when she wrote of stimulating the infant Marianne's attentiveness to objects in her environment.

11.   Gaskell and Holland would probably have agreed with Queen Victoria's statement concerning the eight-year-old Princess Royal:

> I am quite clear that she should be taught to have a great reverence for God, for religion, but that she should have the feeling of devotion and love which our Heavenly Father encourages His earthly children to have for Him, and not out of fear and trembling; that the thoughts of death and an after life should not be represented in an alarming and forbidding view ... (Sir T. Martin, *Life of H. R. H. The Prince Consort* II; qtd. in Burton, p. 36)

12.   Victorian children's literature could reinforce such religious anxiety. The nine-year-old Anglican heroine of *The Fairy Bower* (1841), by John Henry Newman's sister, Harriet Mozley, ponders the 'existence and character of God ... the fearful sense of the doctrine of eternal punishment; the difficulty of reconciling it with the love of the Almighty Creator' (3rd edn, 1843, pp. 13–14).

13.   See Coveney, whose first chapter is entitled, 'The "Cult of Sensibility" and the "Romantic Child"'. Thwaite also notes Wordsworth's influence upon Victorian perceptions of childhood: 'Heaven was soon to lie about infancy, and the Little Nells and Paul Dombeys of Victorian fiction were in sight' (Thwaite, p. 82).

Persons and places

Edward Holland (1806–75) was the son of Swinton Colthurst Holland (1777–1827), younger brother of Dr Peter Holland of Knutsford and Samuel Holland of Liverpool and Plas yn Penrhyn. Edward inherited the manor, advowson and estate of Dumbleton, near Evesham, in Gloucestershire when his father died. He had a new main house built of handsome Cotswold stone, the elaborate contract for which is dated 9 January 1833. Edward became a major figure in his county, especially in agricultural circles. He was elected as a member of Parliament in 1834, though he was defeated in the general election that followed the accession of Queen Victoria in July 1837.

On 27 April 1832 Edward married Sophia, daughter of Elias Isaac, banker, and his wife Harriet, of Boughton, about two miles from Worcester. Not long after, in about April 1833, Edward's sister Charlotte (born in 1808) married Sophia's brother, John Whitmore Isaac. There were nine children of Edward's first marriage, the three oldest being Harriet Sophia (born in 1834), Edward Thurstan (born 10 February 1836) and Frederick Whitmore (born in 1837). Sophia died in 1851 and Edward married for a second time; four children were born of this marriage.

'Grandmama' was either Anne Holland (née Willets), who died in 1845, or Harriet Isaac (née Whitmore). Cousin Swinton, cousin Coo, Dr M., Mrs Garrard, Captain McInroy, Mrs Wake and the servants have not been identified. The first two could be the children of John and Charlotte Isaac, who had two sons and three daughters and were often visited by Mrs Gaskell at Boughton. Some of *The Life of Charlotte Brontë* was written there. (See *Letters*, nos. 308 and 447b, pp. 411, 907–8.)

Chipping Norton is between Evesham and Oxford, in the London direction. Swinton Holland had also purchased 'The Priory' at Roehampton in Surrey, now in greater London.

The diary

February 10th 1837[1]

Edward Thurstan
[Spring 1836]
   From the first shewed great fear of falling catching and holding tightly
any thing close to his hands —
Corners of eyes appeared at ten days old. —
First smiled as if pleased between 3 and 4 weeks old — 2d smile a week
after — About a fortnight after[2] that time (when six weeks old) began to
smile frequently, — and occasionally to crow. —
At eight weeks began[3] to improve in temper, did not cry for a long time
together as before with *no apparent* reason. — Less passionate — I am
convinced that passion had a good deal to do with his early crying fits —

May
   First began to notice things in the park passing before him —
Likes to look at his Sister; — smiling as he watches her —

July
   Took my finger & put it in his mouth.
Left off his night meal f 1st week —
Likes the sound of his own voice talkg to himself —
Begins to hold out his arms to come to me to be fed —
Perceived that image extends beyond retina. —

August
   Very much pleased with little Harriet's birds. — Looked at them crowed
whenever they chirped.
5th — Tries to clasp any object before him feels for it —
Encreasing much in intelligence the last five days.
Cryed to come to me when not hungry.
27th — Begins to imitate. Makes a motion of the mouth in imitation. —
Put his hands together in imitation of his Sister — *26th*.

Septr 7 months
   Talks to himself as he looks at any thing wh: amuses him. —
Begins to have an idea of handling things. — Tries to put [4] every thing to his mouth.
5th — Shows a great love for colors — *8th* — Has a fine rosy color in his cheeks — Baby weaned.

October age 8 months
   Teazed by his coming teeth — Not liking to be laid down —
Observes a good deal. Sometimes gives a sigh as his Sister did — Puts on often an observg frown —
Fond of pulling his Sisters hair — gives a cunning look as he does it & watches to hear if she cries out. —
2 — A picture of a large rabbit being shewn to him he afterwards looked towards it when asked where the rabbit was — This he did 2 or 3 times.
8th — Goes into a pet when his things are put on, (for the last 2 days). Cannot put any thing to his mouth without first drawing it down his face to find his mouth.
20th — Cut first tooth on lower jaw. —
22nd — 2nd tooth cut in lower jaw. —
Put things immediately to his mouth the end of this month.

November
   Frequently goes into a pet when any toy is taken from him or kept from his mouth —
Always wanting to be on his legs —
Has a very intelligent countenance.
Observes a great deal & looks very wise —
Rolls about on the floor & rolls round from side to side to get near to any object which attracts him —
Opens his mouth to kiss — Very much taken with his cousin Swinton — *15th.*

December
   Claps his hands & shakes his head —
Fond as ever of his Sister — seldom cries when she hurts him or takes any thing from him. —
Phebe tells me he said 'Mow' several times as he looked out of the window at the cows. —
Does not attempt *ta* or any of those sounds. [?]

January 1837
   Says Ba & sometimes tries Papa but does not succeed very well —
Begins to understand what is said to him.

He took a plaything from his Sister and on my telling him to give it back to her he immediately put out his hand & did so. —

7th — If he cannot reach a thing with his hand, tries to push it towards him with a stick or any thing with which he is playing —

Having dropped the lid of a box while sitting on my knee he picked it up again by putting a stick with which he was playing inside the lid & lifting it up with the stick until he got it within reach of his hand when he took it off — He looked much pleased at this and dropped it again to repeat the experiment. —

Says 'Papa' 'Pat' for Patty,⁵ 'Ta', 'Bow-wow' & listens attentively to you when you try to teach him a new sound. —

18th — Does not show quite so much generosity as his Sister did at his age in giving away what he has to eat — Will always offer some to Nina & sometimes gives [?] a bit when he is asked for it especially to his Sister. — *19th* — Got up by the side of his tub till he stood upright while lying down close to it — *26th*.

February 1837 [one year old]

Improves in saying words & in walking.

Cries more often when not pleased, this may very much arise from an irritating tooth rash which he now suffers from —

March

Shows more passion & self will — (especially since Phœbe has been away) —

Tries to say many sounds, and becomes far more intelligent.

Always cries when Missie does —

Put out his hand & said 'go away' as his Sister came near him while he was playing — Says 'Up' 'down' 'dog' — Said 'cow' pointing to a picture of one.

23th [*sic*] — Walked alone for some time today — took 1st steps alone about a fortnight since.

23d — While sitting down in my room began to turn over the leaves of his book one by one stopping at all the pictures & talking as he looked at them trying to make me understand 'Bow wow' he repeated looking at a picture of some dogs & then at me — I could not understand all his explanations equally well.

24th — Said to him as he sat on Martha's knee, 'You may go down to the library & dining room.' — Immediately he pushed himself down from her knee & further towards the door of his nursery saying 'go'. —

Tries to say many words.

April

Names of things. — tear[,] he will say as he tears paper —

Understands much that is said & shows he understands it. — *3d.*

Had a quarrel with him in my room because he would crawl to the water tub to get up by it. — Cryed passionately when I took him away & crawled there again. When I again removed him he threw himself back crying; I let him lie on the carpet until finding that he rubbed his head, I put him to lie on the bed — *5th* —

Has never yet shewn any disposition to *revenge* — Tho' often struck by his Sister he has never resented it —

His rash much more irritating, I conclude from his teeth[.] Obliged to give him Castor oil twice. — *13th*

Saw first instance of slyness, finding that he might not touch my water tub to get up by it, he pointed to the flowers upon it & talked as if admiring them very much pointing till his finger touched & then moving his hand to the top to get up, talking to me still. — This he repeated two or three times, in the hope of having his own way — *16th*

Purses up his mouth when vexed or surprised & cries 'Oh — Oh' — The first time I saw him do this, was when Phœbe took his Sister to bed leaving him with me at Chipping Norton. — *17th*

A very good Boy on his journey to London.

18th — Would not kiss his Sister who had in some way been unkind to him when she wished to make it up — This is the first instance I have seen of angry feeling towards her, or of any thing like revenge on his part. He is a most loving admiring Brother. Tho' Missy still cannot get over a jealous feeling towards him.

Says 'Cuckoo' & tries to repeat — Cherry tree.

21st — Is less willing to go to strangers than formerly —

Took him into the string of carriages in Bond St. Was much delighted & said 'how do' to every fresh horse that passed & galloped & made a noise to the horses to go on 'tric-tric' — *24th*

May 1837

It is three weeks since I first heard him attempt any thing like a tune. He did so singing in imitation of Phœbe — 'Rat tat' & since then he frequently sings notes. His voice is a very pretty soft one. — *6th*

Took him to the Surrey Zoological. — He looked surprised but not frightened by the animals. — The birds pleased him but especially a common cock — 'Cock cock' he repeated as he looked at the birds & sometimes 'Cuckoo'. — *6th*

1 year & 3 months old

Saw Dr M: 3 days after he had lanced his gums[.] Shewed no sign of fear or dislike, but laughed when he played with him & did not even shrink when he put his fingers in Bro's[6] mouth. Pretends to read. — Imitates some of the cries 'Old Clo:' etc. —

Very much disappointed to find that Papa was not rolled up in the bed curtains this morning, where he often has hidden himself when the children come in

13th — Says 'Dust-O —' 'Plis'[7] for please. —

Does not give up every thing to his Sister as before, tho' about his own playthings, or any thing he has to eat he is very generous —

Very fond of getting his Sister's playthings, especially any thing she does not like to give up to him.

Very fond of Papa — Constantly calls for him. — He seldom calls Mamma tho when with me he does not always like going away. —

Cut 1st double tooth on lower gum.

22nd — Crawls quickly from one place to another but does not walk so well as when he left Dumbleton. — His tooth rash has thrown him back so much in this respect. —

Often will not take Sissie's hand to walk Calls her 'Siss' —

June

Found 2 double teeth cut today. — one of these must have come thro the skin 3 or 4 days ago —*2nd*

Bro' walks by himself when he holds his own pinafore which is held up for him, or a gown or apron — *3d*

Making progress in walking — Will try to say almost any word or sound that is repeated to him of one syllable, sometimes will try more.

4th & 5th — Very fond of some pigeons that he feed[s] from the windows; & of horses —

Came up to me 'Where Papa' — *8th* — Papa having gone to London the day before.

Walks about alone without any fear.

9th — Walks & runs & does not like being held.

Cut 4th double tooth. Rash appeared again but not very irritating —

12th — Rash better. — seems to feel the hot weather one or two passion- ate cries today — *16th*

Imitates his Sister very much —

Pretends to talk to her. Is not comfortable if away from her for any length of time.

27th — Do not think he remembered his nursery on his return to Dum- bleton.

July

Knocked down the round table in the nursery with the basons of bread & milk upon it & while his Sister cryed over the broken basons & spilt breakfast, he shewed every sign of delight at the mischief he had occa- sioned, laughing and jumping about. —

Very fond of climbing a stool, chair, the steps by my bed or any thing he can reach. —

Pushes his Sister, at the moment She yields to him & sometimes cries & says 'Bo push me' but love of power, generally succeeds, & she goes to him & pulls him down, he resists while he can, colours, & at last when he cannot get her arms away from him gives a cry — According to present appearances he will soon be the Master — *16th*

Seeing Mrs Garrard's Baby put his fingers in his mouth said repeatedly 'Blank-blank' meaning[8] blanket wh he always has in his hand when he puts his own fingers in his mouth to go to sleep —

Asks to be played to. —

Cut one of eye teeth.

20th — Missie was coaxing Phebe & called her her nurse and said, Phebe was her nurse before she was Bro's[9] — Bro hearing this went up tried to push her (Missie)[10] away & said as plainly as he could 'My nurse my nurse'. Can say 'very bad' 'very cruel'. —

Very fond of Nina will give away any thing he has to him [her?]. He does not seem at all greedy.

August [1837]

Has taken a fancy to imitate his Sister about eating, and if she refuses her breakfast or supper he does the same. If she asks to drink he will also, & will lie down or sit up as she does

This is not the case when with me at dinner.

When[11] first he saw Baby he kissed it & whenever he came to my room looked for it & seemed disappointed if he did not find him in my bed. — Cannot bear to see Martha take him.

Altho he never had shewn any thing like greediness before, he twice the[12] end of this month refused to take some nice thing that was offered to him because he thought his piece not so large as his Sister's. — (Once I saw him do so,) — and went without it. —

Is always ready to give away some of what he is eating — and only with his musical toy have I seen him refuse to lend any thing to his Sister. —

Very fond of music, & seems to take much pleasure in colours. —

Can say any thing and often speaks a sentence distinctly —

Is very independant [*sic*] & fears nothing, will climb any thing and very seldom[13] cries when he hurts himself.

[End of first notebook. It seems likely that the missing notebook followed at this point]

Edward Thurstan [on inside of cover]
[Autumn 1838]

Often asks to kneel down & say prayers, if he seems to wish it I always

kneel with him & say a few words, which he repeats solemnly after me.
— I should say he appears to have more of what I should call religious
feelg than Missie at his age. —

Capt McInroy laughed at some little slip or misfortune wh he had —
Me don't like that Gentleman; but 2 days after he seemed to have forgotten his dislike.

Says since our return home a little lesson a few letters now each day.
We began our lesson by imitating the cries of animals picking out a few
from Noah's Ark. —

Was telling him the story of Daniel — 'Me would shoot the lions with
mine gun' & afterwards he said he 'would whip the naughty people with
his coachmans whip'. —

He is now putting together a map [?] with Sissie 'Let I do it' — 'Me can't
do it.' —

Has quite left off sucking his fingers 'Me a coachman. Me not suck mine
fingers.' —

October.

Took very much to Cousin Coo — as he does to most of his lady
cousins —

Talks a great deal to Missie — one day in my room, he was [14] calling
'Moses, Moses' 'Will Moses hurt me Teddy'? Missie asked 'No Moses
won't hurt you'. — 'Is Moses good man Teddy'? [']No Moses is a dog' &
they then went on pretending to play together with a dog —

He is constantly now imitating, calling himself some character, Mr Newman in his boat, a coachman, or some imaginary person. —

Is very fond of saying his lesson, but has not any thing like the memory
of Missie[.] Round O and crooked S are the only two letters I can feel
sure he will know — The differences of form wh Missie when once they
were pointed out to her never forgot, seem to make little impression on
him —

Has given up the coachman and now calls himself a schoolboy —

Phœbe one day when Missie was at prayers in the dining room sent [15]
Thurstan in not knowing that prayers were going on to call Missie —
He walked up to her & stayed silent for a minute & then said 'Phœbe
wants you Missie' — Missie went on kneeling quietly. Thurstan repeated
his message & still finding it unattended too **[sic]** said 'but you must come
Missie for Phœbe wants you['] — When his Papa said to him afterwards,
You should not have talked while we were at prayers, he answered 'But
Phœbe told me to bring Missie' —

He some time before this was saying his prayers to me. I said for him
to repeat Pray God take care of me & — he interrupted me saying 'But
I seed the old woman coming' What old woman dear —'The old woman
you know Mamma.' — I talked to him for some time, but it did not appear

that he was frightened by her image. It was then 10 o'clock & he must have been dreaming, but as I found him awake he would not be happy without saying his prayers to me —

When at our prayers one night he stopped me 'Not say Lizzabeth' I suppose he repented this for the next night he asked me 'Say Lizzabeth, Mamma'.

January 1839

Seemed much to enjoy talking with me & Missie of the delights of heaven, & the beautiful angels that live there, & what he would do when he got there. —

Repeats most things that Missie says. — 'I will walk with the pretty [16] angels in heaven' Missie says, & Teddy immediately says & 'I will walk with the pretty angels too Mamma'. —

In their conversations together [17] Missie prompts him. Will you do this & that, Teddy — Sometimes he says 'No' — but far more generally answers — 'Yes I will do this or that['].

February
10th three years old Measured ft 3 — 1 Inch.

Can say nearly all his large letters & a few of the small & tho sometimes rather inattentive likes saying his lesson very much.

Since his return home he has improved exceedingly & shows much more of his old fine noble character — In his Papa's room he seems inclined to tease Missie & make a noise — Thurstan I said, I think you are inclined to be a little bit naughty, if you want to make a noise you may go to the nursery & make as much as you like & when you feel quite good come down again — 'Yes me is a little bit naughty' I will go to the nursery Mamma' — As he left the room I said 'If you like better to stay in the hall you may do so —' & knock at the door when you feel quite good 'Yes, I will stay in the hall'.

I shut the door & he ran round the hall makg good use of his lungs & then knocked at the door & told me he was good —

Find the children use odd terminations to the verbs — Teddy told me 'I *drinked* [18] some water' & Missie talks of the things GMamma *gaven* her. —

I was shewing Teddy a picture of Adam & Eve in Mant's Bible. Who are those? 'Adam and Eve being turned out of the garden' he told me. — 'See he has got a stick' pointg to the sword in the angel's hand — I told him what it was & pointing to the figure of the angel asked him who it was 'God' he answered — No dear I said, it is an angel. [19] We cannot see God — Nobody has seen God, so we cannot draw a picture of Him — but if we love God when we die we shall see God for we shall go to heaven & then we shall see Him. — 'Will our bodies go to heaven when we die'?

he asked. — I tried to make him understand a difference between body
& soul & told him that Jesus Christ would come again & would then take
our bodies to heaven — I did not know what could have led to this question & asked Martha, who said that he often talked about those sort of
things, when Missie & himself were playing together, & that morng she
heard them talking of Cain & Abel & Missie was telling him how naughty
it was of Cain to kill his Brother — In the picture Missie had seen there
is the body of Abel on the ground wh led me to say some thing on the
subject.

24th — Knows his own blanket & cannot bear another 'O it is mine own
blank' he cried with delight when at Hallow. —

He looked over the sofa 'O look Mamma there is a elephant behind
the sofa look Mamma' I looked & laughed seeing that a basket below had
pushed the cover forward — (He is fond of imagining, makg the glasses at
dinner 'the Papa' 'the Mamma' & [']this is their little Sammy'.) I thought
he was amusing himself in the same way — He was sitting at one end of
the sofa cutting paper afterwards, I was at the other end with my feet up
& Missie close to me — He came so near to Missie as to push her against
my feet. Move to your own end I said to him — 'No the lions are there'
I thought this was a little wish of having his own way, & again told him
to go to his own end. But I fancy imagination was strongly at work. He
repeated what he before said, & looked so serious, that I saw I was wrong
in what I first told him.

27th — On[20] Sunday the two eldest go down to prayers & afterwards
have toast & egg with Papa. Sunday frocks on for dinner & Bible[21]
pictures told them by Mamma —

March 1839

I have since seen several times in other things the strength of imagination. He will say some thing in a very animated way 'Teddy you are
pretending.' — 'No I not pretending' he will answer. —
Afraid of his old tooth rash reappearing.

11th — Two spots now on his head, some times disturbed at night —

17th — His old animation & expression of countenance returning —

Found Swinton & himself breaking the animals of the Noah's Ark,
checked them at first but remembering Edgeworth's opinion of playthings
I said if you wish to break any more you must bring them to me & ask
leave to do so. Thurstan brought some, I consented & heard Swin say
'Now we will kill this one' & talking of breakg their legs. —

I let him be in the room when I tell Missie any new idea about religion —

Broke the legs & head of an ostrich because he wanted the body for an
egg, & was discomposed that he could not get the tail off too. He was
cross after dinner, havg had no morng sleep. I sent him to run round the

hall. Missie joined him, in a short time I heard the fire stirred & on going there found Teddy with the poker in his hand stirring the wood fire & Missie standg by lookg pleased at[22] what he was about. I told them they should both go up & sit in the nursery. Missie skipped up stairs shewg no sign of carg for her punishment. Teddy cryed & would not go up — I sent Phœbe to carry him up stairs — made them sit apart for some time & afterwards told them a story of a child being burnt. —

31st — On going down again to the hall, I told him I hoped he would never touch the poker again, 'But it was so miserable' he said speakg of the fire.

April 1839 3 years 2 m:

Was repeating 'God is at my home' in a very irreverent manner — I checked him — What do you mean? 'God is at my home['] — [']My Father is at my home.[23] God is my Father you know.' — Yes, I answered, [']God is your father but when you speak of God you must speak seriously' — 'But God is at my old home you know, the home that I came from.' Where does God live I asked seriously. 'God lives in heaven, — heaven is my home' —

Heaven will be your home when you die, for if you love God He will take you to heaven to live with him & Papa & Mamma too if they love God. It will be such a beautiful happy home in heaven. 'But' said Missie, 'if we are naughty God will not take us to heaven.' — Not if we do not try to be good, I said. One of the children, Teddy I think asked Does[24] God love us when we are naughty? — God loves us even when we are naughty, but not so much as when we are good.

'Does God love us when we are a little bit naughty Mamma?' Missie asked.

2nd April — Not so obedient as usual and more cross — (East winds perhaps & being kept a good deal in the house) Asked Phœbe whether they had been good 'I was naughty', Thurstan said — *11th*

Gave him a picture of Falstaff & Anne Page. He asked me 'Is that God'? pointg to the mans figure.

17th — Playing with Missie Fred came for some of their things & gave Missie a push by wh her hand was a little hurt from knocking against a chair; Thurstan seeing this immediately gave Fred a strong push which sent him to the floor, Fred began to cry & Thurstan reddened & looked vexed at what he had done. (Fred looked to me for pity, upon which I told him he ought not to have pushed Missie, saying at the same time that Thurstan should not have pushed him quite so hard because he was a little Baby. — I like this spirit of Thurstan for he does not defend himself — *21st*

Missie was sent to tell me he was a dirty boy one morng after he went to bed for his midday sleep. I found that at almost regular distances round the wooden edge of his crib he had been spitting — This is a favourite entertainment of the young gentleman's if he can get a thimble or any other such small appropriate article —

May 1839

Found him crying, askd the reason & seeing at once that he was being punishd for some naughtiness, said I would not ask if he did not wish — he said he did wish me to ask, & told me he was cryg because Phœbe had put him in the corner — Why did she put you in the corner? 'Because I was a naughty boy & teazed Missie.' —

I had found fault with some little naughtiness. Now, my dear children run out of the room I said to the three. As Teddy passed me he said 'Is me your dear boy'? I kissed him & told him he was 'And does you love me'? & he went out lookg very happy. —

Told him of the caterpillar butterfly &c that the butterfly laid its eggs & died. 'Does Jesus Christ come[25] to take their bodies to Heaven'? Teddy asked.

June 1839

Come & give me a kiss my boy I said one day that he came down to dinner — He came to me but before I kissed[26] him said 'I was not a good boy in bed' Did you make a noise? 'No but I got up.' — A day or two before I had kissed him for being a good boy in bed.

7th — Mrs Wake called, her little boy (about 5 years old) kissed Swinton & I believe Bro' when he left. Thurstan came forward for a kiss but the little boy turned round quickly & went away — The colour mounted in Thurstan's cheeks & he looked ready to cry; someone seeing this remarked it aloud, so I thought it better since he knew he[27] was observed to tell him to go down & ask the little boy to kiss him before he got into the carriage. His Cousins hearg this ran down, & got to the hall before Thurstan, so I followd him & when the boy got out of the carriage to kiss the children the cousins being 1st got the first kisses, while Thurstan stood[28] a little behind, lookg anxiously but still keeping back.

21st — The night of our return I said while hearing his prayer — 'Thank you O God for bringing us back safe to Dumbleton' — he asked me afterwards 'Why did God bring us back safe'? Because he loves you very much I said — 'Must we send a letter to the skies? Must we send to God'? —

I told him that God heard all we said, that we need not write. He then asked 'Will[29] God keep us safe from the lions'? 'When we are walking out of doors'? I said there were no lions living in this country that God had not made them to live here — 'But are there lions in Grandmamma's country'? — 'But I do pretend there are lions'.

I talked to him for some time of the care of God & of the country where the lions live.

22nd — Our dear boy has never yet recovered his illness — Probably he never will again possess that daring courage which he showed before. His nerves have been weakened and tho' his *moral courage* is not in the least diminished, he has not the same amount of physical courage. I see this when he is[30] with other children & often I perceive it in an increased sensibility greater than a child of his age should possess. — And which if encouraged may become a source of misery to him thro' life. — I never I believe should appeal to his affections in askg any thing.

Very troublesome in not lying down in the middle of the day — After speakg to him repeatedly I gave him two minutes saying if he did not by that time lie quiet I should punish him — I then called Martha & told her to undress him — 'Are you go[ing] to whip me? What shall you whip me with'? I told him I should have his nightgown put on — 'But I shall be so cold' crying —

I left him having drawn the curtains close round him and found on returng at 1 o'clock that he had been up & down as before & peepg thro the curtains — Told him that as he was still doing as he was bid not he must not go down to dinner with the other children. 'But I shall be so hungry I shall be so very hungry Mamma'.

Then you shall have a piece of bread — 'I should like that' he said lookg pleased — I brought him the bread wh he laid down & eat. After finishg it he got up & down again but did not ask for dinner —

He had got into so restless a state that I felt it better to let him go down without further punishment. Very naughty for some day[s] squeaking if Missie or Fred touched his playthings & often teazg them.

July 26th — Noah's Ark —

[End of notebook]

Notes

1. Written on the inside of the front cover. However, Thurstan was born in 1836; admitted Trinity College Cambridge 5 June 1854, aged 18. Dates have been italicized. Those repeated in notebook headlines have been omitted, but a few have been given in square brackets where the MS is deficient or unhelpful.
2   Altered from 'before'.
3. Altered word.
4. Altered word.
5. Doubtful readings: initial letters altered.
6. Doubtful reading.
7. Doubtful, altered reading.
8. Last two words altered; doubtful reading.
9. Altered word.

10. Inserted word.
11. Follows deletion of 'Altho I have[?]'
12. Follows deletion of word(s).
13. Two words written over deletion of 'never'.
14. Altered word; doubtful reading.
15. Word written over deletion of 'opened the'.
16. Inserted word.
17. Inserted word.
18. Doubtful reading.
19. Last four words inserted.
20. Follows deletion of 'I have'.
21. Inserted word.
22. Three words inserted over deletion of 'encouragg him'.
23. Altered word.
24. Altered word.
25. Follows deletion of 'take their bodies to heaven'.
26. Altered word.
27. Last two words inserted.
28. Inserted word.
29. Altered word.
30. Last two words inserted.

Appendices

INTRODUCTION

Appendices I and II are taken from a quarto manuscript booklet, labelled 'Granny's "Recollections" and some letters JGR', in the possession of Miss Barbara Hartas Jackson. We are grateful to her for allowing it to be consulted at Manchester College, Oxford, and to the Chaplain and Librarian for making appropriate arrangements.

The booklet measures 9 × 7¼" and has soft, marbled covers. Forty leaves, ten of them blank, are stitched in the middle; watermark, 'VALLEYFIELD' in open caps. It contains fair copies of several items: pages [1–8] hymns by JGR; [9–48] letters from Scotland in July 1835 by JGR; [49–59] 'Recollections of a long life'. On page [46] the hand of the copyist changes and is identical with that of the 'Recollections'.

The autograph of Appendix III, two folio leaves folded, addressed and sealed, is unavailable. It is printed here from a slightly defective photocopy of it in Chapple's possession, omissions being supplied from a typed transcript, courtesy of the Librarian of the Literary and Philosophical Society of Newcastle.

Appendix IV is reprinted from volume 1 of the Knutsford Edition, *The Works of Mrs. Gaskell,* ed. A. W. Ward, 1906, pp. xxvi–xxvii. The poem's present location is unknown.

The autograph of Appendix V, first printed in *Letters,* Appendix F, is now on loan deposit in the Brotherton Library, Leeds.

Quotations from Appendices I and III appeared in J. A. V. Chapple, 'Unofficial lives: Elizabeth Gaskell and the Turner family', in Charles Parish, *The History of the Literary and Philosophical Society of Newcastle upon Tyne,* Volume II, 1896–1989 (Newcastle upon Tyne, 1990), pp. 106–20, but neither text has been published in full till now.

PERSONS AND PLACES

Mary Robberds was the oldest child of the Reverend William Turner of Newcastle and born, according to his register of births and baptisms, on 24 February 1786. She married the Reverend John Gooch Robberds (1789–1854), minister of Cross Street Unitarian chapel in Manchester, in 1811. 'Recollections of a long life' must have been composed some time after 1866 – it refers to the death of the 'hireless preacher', Travers Madge – and before her own death in 1869.

William Turner (1761–1859), minister of Hanover Square Unitarian chapel in Newcastle from 1782, married Mary, daughter of Thomas Holland of

Manchester. They had a family of five boys and two girls, Mary dying about three months after the birth of her youngest child Ann on 21 October 1796. In 1799 Turner married Jane, eldest daughter of the Reverend William Willets of Newcastle under Lyme. Jane's sister Mary had in 1786 become the wife of Peter Holland of Knutsford and the mother of Henry, Mary, Bessy and Lucy; she died in 1803. Their sister Anne married Peter's youngest brother, Swinton Colthurst Holland, in 1805. Such interlocking marriages were typical of the narrow circle of families whose religious beliefs made them unacceptable to Trinitarian Christians.

Two boys of Turner's first marriage, Thomas and John, died very young in the 1790s. Another son, Philip Holland, survived until the age of twenty-one, dying on 22 September 1811. Henry (b. 4 May 1792) married Catharine (b. 21 February 1797), daughter of John Cole and Catharine Rankin of Newcastle. Henry became Unitarian minister at Nottingham, but died young in 1822. Turner's oldest son and namesake (b. 13 January 1788) was tutor in mathematics at Manchester College, York, from 1810 until he was called to be Unitarian minister at Halifax in 1829; he was an executor of Mrs Hannah Lumb's will with Edward Holland of Dumbleton. There were no children of Turner's second marriage. Mrs Jane Turner died aged 68 in 1826, many years before her husband and Ann Turner (1796–1850).

William Gaskell became John Robberds' junior colleague at Cross Street chapel in 1828. Mrs Gaskell, then Elizabeth Stevenson, is said to have spent the winters of 1829–30 and 1830–31 in the home of Turner and his unmarried daughter Ann, who were living at this time in a superior district of Newcastle, Clavering Place, having moved from Cumberland Row. She is also said, without positive evidence, to have first met the Reverend William Gaskell at the Robberds' house in the rural area of Greenheys, near Manchester. By this time, as the 'Recollections' reveal, the Robberds had moved to Grosvenor Square, Oxford Road, then on the edge of the town.

Though brief and randomly selective, Mary Robberds' 'Recollections' provide numerous parallels to Elizabeth's own youth and upbringing in comfortable middle-class Unitarian circles – in which, nevertheless, a provocative author like Mary Wollstonecraft was read and even admired. There was a copy of her *Thoughts on the Education of Daughters, With Reflections on Female Conduct in the More Important Duties of Life* (1787) in the vestry library at Hanover Square chapel. Her more famous *A Vindication of the Rights of Women*, actually quoted in Turner's letter, appeared in 1792.

Mrs Robberds' simple 'Recollections', taken in conjunction with the letter of advice her father sent to her, give a very strong indication of what was expected of Elizabeth Gaskell on her marriage to a Unitarian minister in 1832. In Elizabeth's first letter to Turner after her marriage, dated from 1 Dover Street, Oxford Road, on 6 October 1832, she demurely promised to be 'one who intends to try' to be a 'useful friend' to the families of the Cross Street congregation. 'My dear colleague too', she wrote, 'has promised her assistance and advice with regard to my duties' (not in *Letters,* but printed in full by Chapple, 'Unofficial Lives', in Parish, pp. 107–8).

The Robberds' daughter Mary Jane, for whose children the 'Recollections' were composed, married Charles Herford in May 1852 (*Letters,* no. 126, p. 191), and was responsible for one of the first obituaries of Mrs Gaskell, published in *The Unitarian Herald* (edited by William Gaskell) for 17 November 1865. In this she states that Mrs Gaskell mainly devoted herself in the early years of her marriage to the instruction of her daughters, 'whom she brought up most tenderly', but:

> steadily and consistently objected to her time being considered as belonging in any way to her husband's congregation for the purposes of congregational visiting, and to being looked to for that leadership in congregational work which is too often expected of 'the minister's wife;' but, at the same time, there have been few who have been more willing than she was to give time, and thought, and trouble where she felt they would be of any service ...

Mrs Mary Herford was in an excellent position to judge the quality and nature of her response over the years.

Robberds' consolatory hymn and Elizabeth Gaskell's tender sonnet speak for themselves. More informally, her 'Precepts for the guidance of a Daughter' display a sense of irony that might also be latent in Mary Robberds' annotation on Turner's beautifully written letter, 'My Father's Pastoral Epistle', and a love of fun that can be seen in the scribble around its edges, quite possibly by Mrs Jane Turner.

1. Mary Robberds, 'Recollections of a long life'

Being asked to write some account of my life, I replied that I had nothing amusing to tell, & I was afraid it would be very dull. 'Oh no it won't' said my little grandson. Well I will try.

In my father's house there was no girl but me, the other children were boys – so I played at Boys' games. There was a little[1] brook running in a valley not far off, & there we played at making mud pies & damming up the water, & sailing small boats. I was about four years old, and I am afraid I was not a very tidy little girl. I was very fond of singing, & I remember an old lady giving me a gold band for my head[2] hat, for singing 'God save the King'.

I suppose we were a troublesome set of children to my mother for when I was five years old, a kind friend took me to live with her for a year at another Newcastle, – Newcastle-under-Lyne [sic] in Staffordshire. As I had no brook to paddle in and had to learn to read, I daresay I was naughty sometimes for I remember being sent to a room by myself to learn my letters. But I soon found that I could hear the church bells chime, & I liked listening to them better than learning my letters. Some things, however, I liked very much, for I often saw Mr Wedgwood – the famous Mr [Josiah] Wedgwood – and he took me to see the potteries where plates & cups were made. When I returned home, I had learnt to read, & was very happy with my mother, & little brothers –

At eight years of age I went to a boarding school at Manchester, and was taught by my Uncle who was very clever, though quite blind [Thomas Holland, brother of the Reverend John Holland of Bolton]. He could hear very quickly, & soon found out if any of the girls tried to deceive him. If they pretended to read the figures of their sums different from what they had written he took hold of their slate & rubbed them all out; of course it was only naughty girls who tried to cheat[3] him. I stayed at school two years & learnt Geography & History & Arithmetic as Amy & Minnie do.

My holidays were often spent at a very pleasant place in the country called Sandlebridge. It was a fine large[4] old house covered in front with a vine; a flower garden & grass court sloped down from the house to a lane in which grew large elm & oak trees; at the back of the house there was a kitchen garden, & at the side a small garden containing bee hives – but the thing we children liked best was a sand heap where we could play at building houses without making our frocks dirty. In the yard there was a pump and poultry & a pigsty, & beyond was the dairy where often [we] saw butter & cheese made – In the farm yard we saw the cows milked & the calves fed & sometimes hid in the hayfield. Down the lane there was a mill for grinding the corn, turned by a large water wheel, & near it was a smithy, where we were fond of standing to see the smith blow with his large bellows, & make horseshoes – tires for cart wheels &c.

When it rained there was plenty of amusement in the house. Besides playing at 'I spy' there was a game called shuffleboard in the dining room or houseplace, where we generally sat. It was played by pushing flat round pieces of coin into a well at the end of the board – something like playing at a bagatelle board, only instead of balls we pushed flat pieces. Then as I said the old house was a capital place for playing hide & seek, for there were two staircases and different ways into the rooms, to hide in. There were two clocks one in the house place, which struck the hours very quickly, the other on the staircase which struck so slowly that it was said a man might go to sleep and have a dream between the first & last stroke of twelve. Out of doors there was no end of amusement, besides cows & pigs & horses there were chickens & pigeons and a large barn where we could cover ourselves with hay & there was a pond where we sometimes saw the sheep washing. All this was very delightful.

When I was ten years old, my dear mother died, so for a few years, I went to a day school at Newcastle, whilst a kind old lady took care of us at home. Then my father married again, & we had a kind & good mother – She taught us how to employ our time usefully, & not waste it in nonsense, & yet she liked fun as well as any body, & was very entertaining; she encouraged us in learning to draw, & often read to us while we were at work. But she often locked up the book when she had done, till the next evening, because, she said, it was an idle habit interrupting our work to finish a story, &[5] it was a good exercise of patience to wait, we rather rebelled at this, but I daresay she was right. In this manner we went on for several years very happily: when I was about eighteen years of age, I went several pleasant & improving journies.

First to London for three months, during which time I was a guest six weeks at Mr John Wedgwoods a son of the Mr Wedgwood mentioned above. Mrs Wedgwood & her governess Mrs Learon were very kind to me & took me[6] to see many curious & beautiful things. My kind father allowed me to have[7] a few good lessons in drawing & singing. They were very expensive so I tried to get as much good as I could out of them; often thinking, as I took my lesson, here is half a guinea going, I must get as much improvement as I can.[8]

I afterwards had a very pleasant visit at Mr Carle [?], and attended lectures at the Royal Institution, and enjoyed a great deal of very pleasant society; among other remarkable people, I frequently saw Mrs [Anna Letitia] Barbauld & Dr [John] Aikin, who were so kind to me that I began to think I must be remarkable. But my vanity was soon[9] seasonably checked, for one day on Miss Aikin saying to her father, 'Here is Miss Turner' he made a low bow – but when she added, 'Papa, it is Miss Turner of Newcastle', he came and shook hands with me, and afterwards invited me to stay at his house for a few days. This taught me that it was not for myself but because I was the daughter of a man so beloved & honoured as the Revd Mr Turner. I never forgot this lesson.

On my return home, I was so happy as to be able to make my drawing lessons useful to my dear father; for he had been appointed lecturer to the 'Literary & Philosophical Society' and my mother encouraged me to draw the diagrams on the black board, which he wanted as illustrations of his subject. As I could do them privately before the lecture there could be no objection, & I quite enjoyed the work; it also enabled me better to understand the lecture. –

This was a very pleasant part of my life as my brothers were clever & amusing companions and my cousin Henry Holland who lived some years with us, was a great favourite, & his sisters also paid us long visits. My mother, who as I have said was very amusing, promoted our improvement & happiness. My little sister Ann was quite a little child & very delicate & required a great deal of care; but my mother made even this entertaining. One day when she was standing at the window reading, she said 'Mother, who are my fellow creatures? [' '] Why look out of the window, & whoever you see are your fellow creatures.' 'What! those lime people Mother?' 'Yes, certainly!' said my Mother. 'Not fellows like stockings' replied Anne. Another time on a gentleman coming to tea my Mother said, 'Anne ask for candles'. 'What –dles Mother[?]' We usually burnt only one candle.[10] My cousin Mary Holland, whom you now know as Cousin Mary at Knutsford staid a year with us, and was then as now, very amusing. There was a great storm of wind one night, which blew down the brickwork of a built up window in the room where we slept. I said to her 'Don't be frightened Mary it is nothing'. 'Bother, but it is though' she said 'for I feel them' and truly the bricks had fallen actually upon her, as she lay in bed; but she was not hurt at all. My Mother was clever in checking any kind of vanity. If I fancied myself pretty, she once said 'Pretty: why you have a cadaverous complexion & a cantankerous skin.' We were always required to write a remembrance of the sermon on a Sunday, & to read it aloud after tea. We did not much like this, but we were obliged to do it; & my Father & Mother always made the evening pleasant for us by singing & talk –

When I speak of Newcastle, I can never forget a family who, next to our own, formed the greatest part of our happiness. This was the family of Ranins. They lived in a large house at the Forth, at that time a very pleasant residence, having a large garden, & very near a square of large trees. The view across the river was also[11] very pretty. It is now occupied by the Railway Station. But we had many a happy day there. The Miss Rankins sympathised in all our happiness, and at last our families were more closely & happily united by the marriage of their niece Catharine Rankin to my dear Brother Henry Turner:– But I am going on too fast.

Before the event last mentioned took place, I was invited to visit Mrs [Catherine] Cappe of York. As this was the occasion of a very important event in my life, I must give you some account of my visit: Mrs Cappe was an old lady, who took a great interest in education, & wrote many pamphlets on the subject. But her principal subject was the College for the prepera-tion of young men for the ministry at that time settled in York under the care of the Revd C. Welbeloved. In this institution Mrs Cappe took the warmest interest. Her respect & regard for Mr Welbeloved was unbounded, and she took a sincere interest in the students, expressing her approval when they did right, & her censure when she thought them wrong. They sometimes smiled at her interference but in after life it had its effect. My Brother William & Mr [John] Kenrick were the Tutors, so of course I saw & heard a great deal of college talk, & saw several of the students particularly Mr Robberds & Mr [James] Yates who were reckoned the cleverest.

Mr Robberds was early distinguished as a preacher: and sometimes Mrs Cappe, with whom I sat at chapel would rise from her seat when she par-ticularly liked the sermon, & said in a whisper 'very good'. The young men were very kind and attentive to me, taking me to look at the noble minster & the Museum Gardens, & we had often very pleasant tea parties at my Brother's lodgings. All this was very pleasant, & I should have enjoyed my visit very much – but by degrees I made a discovery which gave me great uneasiness, & which has influenced the whole of my subsequent life. I found that I was growing deaf. At first I hoped that it was only accidental, and my friends encouraged me to consult aurists, in the hope that it might be merely some obstruction in the ear. But it was no use – and after a few years I was obliged to rest content with any alleviation I could obtain from the use of a trumpet. This has been the trial of my life, but I was not fully aware of it till some time after I had been married to Mr Robberds, your Grandfather.

After leaving York I went some visits among my relations in Lancashire, to my Uncles at Bolton & Manchester, & afterwards to Liverpool, where I paid a very amusing visit at Dr [Peter] Crompton's at Eton [House, Waver-tree]. He was a warm-hearted generous man, but rather eccentric, and though essentially kind he liked to tease us with his tricks. We were a large party of young people in the[12] house, & the Dr professed to keep school every morning, and examine us in what he read – the book was Kaimes' elements of criticism, & Dr Crompton applied to us to translate the Latin & Greek quotations – 'Now, Miss Turner, give us the English [of] this sen-tence' 'Sir! I don't understand Greek': 'Well then, here is a Latin one.' 'I can't, sir. I don't know Latin.' 'Oh never tell me Mr Turners daughter, & not understand Latin'; & so he went on with the rest of us. One day, however, he & Mrs Crompton, who was a charming woman, gave me a great pleasure in taking me to see the celebrated Mr [William] Roscoe. He lived at a beautiful place called Allerton, & his house was adorned with beautiful paintings & statuary. His conversation was a great treat and I enjoyed the evening very much. You know that Mr Roscoe was the author of Leo Xth [1805] and of Lorenzo de Medici [1795], so he was a celebrated man, & there were several other clever men in Liverpool at that time, some of whom I saw, Dr [James] Currie, Dr [William] Shepherd, Mr [John] Yates &c. I like to recollect the visit.

When I was five & twenty I was married and came to live at Manchester. It was rather a dull wedding, for it was on the last day of the year, the ground covered with snow, and of course it was no season for what is called a wedding journey. We merely stopped for one day at York and then went direct to Manchester where my husband had a house in Mosley Street. We lived there ten years, & your uncles, Charles & John were born there. It was no idle life that we lived there. Your Grandfather had a boy's school, and was also minister of a large congregation. Our friends were very kind; I cannot tell you the names of half of them – but the names of [Samuel] Jones, [Thomas] Robinson, [Benjamin and James] Heywood, [Alexander] Henry &c can never be forgotten. Mrs Jones especially, was always ready to help us, whenever we were at a loss.

But notwithstanding this, we had many trials, & the worst was that my husband's health began to give way: after struggling on for some time he determined at length to give up the school, & take a small house in the country, where by economy we might live on our chapel income. We went to live at Greenheys & for three years were very happy, & your Grandfather's health improved. The two boys worked in the garden, & helped in the house, cleaned their own shoes & went errands, for we had only one servant. Soon however a change came, another little boy was born, and our friends persuaded us to move to a larger house near the Town in Grosvenor Square. I was very sorry to leave our pleasant cottage with its large garden.

Still a larger house had its advantages, as we were more within reach of all classes of society and possessed many means of being useful. And here I got the credit of knowing & doing much more than was[13] true; for I often copied out the sermons which were particularly admired; so people said that I *wrote* your Grandfather's sermons, which was a great mistake.

In the course of a few years we were made very happy by the birth of a little girl. We had so wished for one; and we did our best to spoil her, only she was a sweet-tempered little thing & wouldn't be spoiled. I suppose you guess who this was. My deafness was a great hindrance in my teaching her, but after some years her aunt, Mrs Henry Turner, finished what I had so imperfectly begun, & made her what she is. While we lived in Grosvenor

Square Travers Madge came as a student to the Manchester College. Everybody loved him, & he had peculiar influence over the children in the Lower Mosley St School. But indeed he was beloved by everybody, & some said it was a good atmosphere to live in. You all loved him, & there was only one anxiety about him, he had a very uncertain health. Sometimes he felt strong and able to undertake many things in education, for he was very clever – then he broke down & was obliged to give up all the good plans he had formed. At last you know he died.

Another change of abode we had, from Grosvenor Square to Acomb Street, & here I hope we shall remain till my last great change, for I am very happy here with my daughter & my grandchildren.

Notes

1. Inserted word.
2. Deleted word.
3. Word written over cancelled 'teach'.
4. Inserted word.
5. 'when' deleted.
6. Last three words inserted.
7. 'sev' deleted
8. 'could out of them' deleted.
9. Deletion follows; perhaps 'sat upon'.
10. 'Another … candle' inserted as footnote.
11. Inserted word.
12. Word written over deleted 'his'.
13. Inserted word.

II. Revd J. G. Robberds, 'How beautiful is death …'

How beautiful is death
Upon that infant brow!
No sign of pain is there,
No trace of suffering now.

How beautiful is death
In that sweet peaceful smile!
Which shews there ne'er has been
Or word or thought of guile.

How beautiful is death
When we can look and say,
No stain was on the soul
That hence has passed away.

How beautiful is death
When we can look and feel
That soul is now with Him
Who every wound can heal.

III. William Turner to Mary Robberds, Newcastle, 29 January 1812

Address Mrs Robberds / The Rev. J. G. Robberds' / Mosley Street / Manchester / Single
Endorsed 29 Jan. 1812. / Rev. Wm T. *and* January 1812 / My Father's Pastoral / Epistle

Newcastle. Jan. 29. 1812

Though I have followed you in idea, my dearest Mary, almost from hour to hour since you left us, amidst the various scenes through which I pleased myself with supposing you to be passing, I have not thought it necessary or even seasonable to trouble you with either my good wishes or my advice; because I was sure you would give my affection full credit for the former; and because I had no doubt of your conducting yourself, through the various circumstances attendant on your change of character, with that modest and unaffected propriety, which would render the latter quite unnecessary, had I been qualified to offer it in this stage of your proceedings. But now that the ceremonials attending your first introduction are over, and you are beginning to think of settling upon[1] a plain domestic plan, will you allow me to pour forth some of the overflowings of a Father's heart, which has often of late engaged the head to meditate on your future duties and prospects?

On the qualities which a man of sense will most regard in the choice of a wife, you have read the judicious remarks of Dr [John] Aikin; on the general duties of a wife you have availed yourself of the advice of Mr [Thomas] Gisborne; and you have perused the strong and often coarse, though too often well-founded, strictures of Mrs Wollstonecraft. I need not, therefore, say any thing to you on the *general* rights and obligations of Husband and Wife: you are neither of you, I trust, disposed to be jealous of each other's rights, or grudging in the discharge of mutual obligations. You will not be disposed to exclaim with Mrs W. 'Is a wife to be an upper-servant, to provide her husband's meals, and take care of his linen?' [*Vindication*, chapter 3] No: not as an upper servant, but as a companion and helper, to make his home comfortable and his meals pleasant, when he returns from acting the part of a fellow servant in the discharge of those public or more private duties by which he is to make the necessary provision for the common maintenance.

But to have done with generals: it was my object to point out some of those particular duties which may be required from the wife of a Minister connected with such a congregation as that at Manchester. – Such a person may render herself a help meet for her husband in various respects.

In order to form a full idea of all the ways in which she may be so, it is necessary that she carefully consider the nature of his profession; and the ends of it. – No less than the religious and moral improvement of *all* his hearers, in order to their usefulness here, and their happiness hereafter. To answer such important purposes he is not to be a mere lecturer, to make his weekly appearance before them with a set discourse; he is to be their teacher, their exemplar, their friend and counsellor; the mediator between his richer and poorer hearers, the director of their charities for the former, and the consoler of the latter in their distress; the institutor and manager of useful plans for the religious education of the young, and the religious information of persons of all ages; in short, the promoter of religious truth and practice both by precept and example.

In most of these respects he may be materially assisted by his wife: in many she may, with great advantage, be his proxy.

If she be not fitted or disposed to help him in any of them,[2] he is greatly to be pitied, and perhaps even in some degree to be blamed: It is at least a sign that he has made a very injudicious choice. The conduct of a Minister's Wife may often benefit or mislead his flock, almost as much as his own. I have somewhere read that in the Protestant Churches of Hungary a Minister has been degraded 'whose wife has indulged herself in amusements which bespeak the gaiety of a mere lover of the world, rather than the gravity of a Christian Matron': a severity said to be grounded on the supposition 'that the wife, having promised obedience to her husband, can do nothing but what he either directs or approves.' It might have been grounded on the Apostolic precept, that the deaconesses[3] 'must be grave, not slanderers, sober, faithful in all things.' I Tim. III. 11.

A Minister's Wife ought, therefore, to study her husband's reputation, and give weight to his instructions, by her own discreet and prudent conduct. – In the management of her family, aware that she has taken upon herself the task of making a limited income support a respectable appearance, she will study the arts of frugal but decent housekeeping: and will be particularly careful that no needless expences be incurred on her own account.

But this is, comparatively, a trifling object; though by no means to be overlooked. The main object of the Christian Teacher will naturally be, to have his family set an example of attention to religious duties, and of general decorum and propriety of conduct: he will particularly look to his wife for ready and active co-operation in these important particulars. He will be greatly disappointed if she throw any obstacles in the way, if she do not rather cordially join with[4] and even encourage him, in the establishment and maintenance, of family prayer; he will rejoice if she appear disposed to qualify herself for the future education of her own young family, if it should please God to entrust her with such a charge, by previous reading, by personal observation and enquiry, and by an active attention, in the mean time,[5] to the religious and other[6] instruction of the lower classes of the congregation, either in charity and sunday schools, or otherwise; and if she set, in these respects, a good example to the young women in general of her acquaintance. What better preparation can she make for a successful discharge of duty in the education of her own children; who in the natural course of things fall to be almost exclusively[7] the objects of their Mother's attention during that most important period of their lives when those impressions are to be made which are most likely to be lasting, and even to give the prevailing direction to the whole of their future lives!

For this you are, indeed, already better prepared than most young women, by the care and attention you have shewn to the management of our Sunday-School; and by the alacrity with which, even to your marriage-day, you have submitted to be taught, as well as to exert yourself to teach. In both these respects you will, I am sure, continue to set a good example, as far as your situation affords you opportunity: will willingly place yourself on the bench of instruction, under either your husband or Mr Grundy [Reverend John, senior minister]; or will lend your assistance to establish order in any school which may at present subsist, or hereafter be established.

But while you are thus[8] actively religious yourself, and engaged in promoting it among others, you will not forget that you are to help encourage and support your husband, by cultivating a prevailing cheerfulness, both of countenance and heart. In the ordinary course of his multiplied employments, he will often return from the school, the study, or from[9] visits abroad, fatigued and exhausted; let him find his home made comfortable by pleasant looks and cheerful conversation, or by a readiness to join in plans of relaxation by such reading as you can both be interested in. – I hope he will not often, but I cannot flatter him that he will not sometimes, meet with disappointments, from want of success in his public or private schemes, from the behaviour of his friends, either in a general moral respect, or to himself in particular. In such cases you must be his refuge, his comfort and counsellor. In no such cases will you ever aggravate; but soften and conciliate as much as possible. In particular you will study to allay any little resentments he may feel upon such occasions. – This caution may perhaps be particularly necessary in the case of two ministers; for each of whom there will of course be partialities, according to the particular tastes and intimacies of individuals.[10] Your husband is in this respect particularly happy in a colleague, who I trust will always find himself equally happy in him; indeed I persuade myself that there will never be any jealousies or heartburnings, in consequence of preferences which are inevitable, and in themselves perfectly innocent, either between them, or among the members of the congregation. But if anything of this kind should occur, let it be your business never to hear any officious reports that may be suggested to you by well or ill-meaning people: but always study the things that make for peace, and things by which both your husband and his colleague may edify one another, as well as those with whom they are connected. I hardly need to caution you against a proneness to take offence on your own account; or embarrassing your husband with[11] any of your own squabbles. You must alter very [much] before you engage in any.

Neither do I think you are in any great danger of contracting a meddling[12] gossiping habit, or giving countenance or encouragement to those who have. A more[13] mischievous quality can scarcely be imagined: [by] which, instead of becoming her husband's help-meet, a wife contributes more than any thing to his trouble and vexation. I should otherwise be cautious of offering my next piece of advice, to make yourself acquainted with the several members of the congregation, their characters, occupations, habits, wants, &c, &c. I don't mean that you should personally know them all, but the more extensively the better. You can at least learn all the particulars which your husband has collected concerning each in his congregational common-place-book. You will thus become acquainted with all the ways in which they can severally be of use to you, or you can render yourself useful to them; you will also learn by this means who are the persons with whom you can with the greatest mutual advantage deal for the several articles you may want to purchase. For, certainly, all other things being equal, or even nearly so, it is a reciprocity which is only fair and reasonable that you should lay out among the congregation that income which you receive from them. You will thus, as well by a mutual interchange of good offices in other respects, strengthen your husband's interest with his people. Even by knowing their places of abode, and at chapel, you will be prepared to receive and return the civilities of those who will feel entitled to offer them, and not incur the hazard of having it said by any, 'that their minister's wife was too proud to speak to them.' – But you may thus besides have various opportunities of assisting him, and often may even be a preferable substitute: in various cases of sickness, and other circumstances of distress, especially among your own sex, and children, the good offices of a female may be more essentially useful than those of any man. – In various cases, also, of cooperation in the management of certain[14] public charities, as the Repository, the Lying In Charity &c you may also contribute to those personal services which it will be out of your husband's line to offer.* See Mrs Cappe's excellent Paper on Female Visitors in Hospitals, Pamphleteer, No. [space left by WT].

But besides cheerfulness and active cooperation, fidelity to admonish your husband, if any case should occur of neglect or deficiency, and to remind him of his duties, whether general or particular, will never, I persuade myself, be undervalued or ill-received by him. You may indeed be of great use to each other in maintaining your respective provinces regular, by keeping an exact account of the business of each day, and comparing notes, every night before bed-time, of what each has respectively done or omitted doing.

I am far from pretending to claim a right, from having myself observed them, to give either to you now, or to your husband formerly, the advices with which you have each been troubled: but I persuade myself you both will take them in good part; and will believe that there exists no jealousy of either of you excelling as much as you please the friends who have gone before you. In one respect, at least, you have not hitherto learnt to exceed them – the habit of writing long letters: which, between such near and dear friends, we will not allow our neighbour Thompson to call 'silly'. There is, however, a proper limit with regard to all things; and in this instance I fear you will be tempted to think I have exceeded it. With my best love, then, to yourself and your dearest friend, I will at length relieve you by subscribing myself

Your affectionate Father
Willm Turner.

PS. Your letter, just recd gives you a claim to be admitted into the class of long letter writers. But tho' it gives us many interesting particulars, we want a hundred particulars more. You have not answered *one* of our queries, Whether your things among the rest the Ham [15] got safe; and what they (*I* particularize your Mother's preparations for you) have been th[ough]t of? Whether you have bought and sent off the Calico Sheeting? Did you invite MAL [Marianne Lumb?] – Indeed I think you can not have received a New's paper I sent you from hence, explaining to you how you were to seek for what would be written in the Papers from York, viz in the blank space [16] on each side of the Title. – You will by this time have recd, and probably acknowledged, the stupendous piece of work from the Burn. You would not I hope overlook in the unpacking, the seal, of [17] the impression of which on your Mother's long letter, you take no notice. Perhaps my Irish caution came too late. – Lastly, we wish you would not determine to finish a letter whether long or short, at a sitting; but write a little, whenever you have time (beginning with replies to letters recd) and then send it off whenever 'tis finished. More last words! How comes it [18] that your letters are so long in getting to the office? The first is dated 16, and the office mark is 18 recd 20; [19] this last is 25, mark 27, recd 29. – You have sent us no specific direction to you.

[Around the edges of the letter, possibly written by Mrs Jane Turner]
I cannot see you in your new habitation yet. you will think us sad discontented mortals – but we have lost you, crampetes! [20] send Ann the large sheet you promised with plans & drawings & then I will fill you one with pretty agreeable small talk without the least bit of a lecture. I shall have plenty to say for Miss [Lucy] Aikin is coming on friday morning, I hope you will get me the sheeting before Cotton is ris.

Notes

1.   Word written over deleted 'down with[?]'.
2.   Three words written over deleted 'these respects'.
3.   Word inserted over a deletion.
4.   Inserted word.
5.   Last four words inserted.
6.   Last two words inserted.
7.   Inserted word.
8.   Inserted word.
9.   Inserted word.
10. Word written over deleted 'the several members of the congregation'.
11. Word written over deleted 'in'.
12. Inserted word.
13. Word written over illegible deletion.
14. Inserted word.
15. Last five words inserted.
16. Last four words inserted.
17. Inserted word.
18. Inserted word.
19. Last two words inserted.
20. Inexplicable reading.

IV. E. C. Gaskell, 'On Visiting the Grave of my Stillborn Little Girl'

Sunday, July 4th, 1836

I made a vow within my soul, O child,
When thou wert laid beside my weary heart,
With marks of Death on every tender part,
That, if in time a living infant smiled,
Winning my ear with gentle sounds of love
In sunshine of such joy, I still would save
A green rest for thy memory, O Dove!
And oft times visit thy small, nameless grave.
Thee have I not forgot, my firstborn, thou
Whose eyes ne'er opened to my wistful gaze,
Whose suff'rings stamped with pain thy little brow;
I think of thee in these far happier days,
And thou, my child, from thy bright heaven see
How well I keep my faithful vow to thee.

V. E. C. Gaskell, 'Precepts for the Guidance of a Daughter'

1: Remember Evelyn was *not* the first Norman King of England.
2: Wash your hands.
3: *When* you have washed them, hold a book in them.
4: Diminish your calves.
5: Pluck your arms.
6: Don't have the same thing said of you that was said of Master Philip.
7: Get up early, but not *too* early.
8: Talk German so fast that no one can ascertain whether you speak grammatically or no.
9: Don't gobble; it turns maidens and turkey-cocks purple.
10: Remember John Still.
11: Don't talk like Scott and Adsheads' about young men's dress.
12: Forget ties and studs for one *little* week.
13: Don't swear.
14: Assume the power of reading, if you have it not.
15: Hold your book right way up. N.B. you may know which is the right way by examining at what end of a page the numbers occur. Where the numbers are that is the top; to be held *away* from you.
16: Not to make a sequence.
17: Not to leave your room like a hay-field, of which the grass *is* gowns & brushes.
18. Not to take pocket-handkerchiefs for articles of virtue.

Altogether to conduct herself as becomes the daughter of E. C. Gaskell [in Meta's hand:] & sister of M. E. Gaskell.

Bibliography

Richard Altick, *Victorian People and Ideas* (Norton, New York: 1973).

Gillian Avery and Angela Bull, *Nineteenth Century Children: Heroes and Heroines in English Children's Stories, 1780–1900* (Hodder and Stoughton, London: 1965).

Robert Bator (ed.), *Masterworks of Children's Literature*, Vol. 3. Gen. ed. Jonathan Cott (8 vols.; Stonehill Communications and Chelsea House Publishers, New York: 1983).

Isabella Beeton, *The Book of Household Management* (London: 1861).

Felicia Bonaparte, *The Gypsy-Bachelor of Manchester: The Life of Mrs Gaskell's Demon* (UP of Virginia, Charlottesville: 1992). Victorian Literature and Culture Series.

John Bradley and Ian Ousby (eds), *The Correspondence of John Ruskin and Charles Eliot Norton* (Cambridge UP, Cambridge: 1987).

Patricia Branca, *Silent Sisterhood: Middle Class Women in the Victorian Home* (Croom Helm, London: 1975).

Julia Briggs, 'Women writers and writing for children: From Sarah Fielding to E. Nesbit', in Gillian Avery and Julia Briggs (eds), *Children and Their Books: A Celebration of the Work of Iona and Peter Opie* (Oxford UP, Oxford: 1989), pp. 221–50.

Richard H. Brodhead, 'Sparing the rod: Discipline and fiction in antebellum America', *Representations* 21 (1988), pp. 67–96.

Frederick Burkhardt and Sydney Smith (eds), *The Correspondence of Charles Darwin*, Vol. 1 (8 vols.; Cambridge UP, Cambridge: 1985).

Elizabeth Burton, *The Early Victorians at Home, 1837–1861* (Longman, London: 1972).

J. A. V. Chapple, 'Two unpublished Gaskell letters from Burrow Hall, Lancashire', *The Gaskell Society Journal* 6 (1992), pp. 67–72.

J. A. V. Chapple, assisted by John Geoffrey Sharps, *Elizabeth Gaskell: A Portrait in Letters* (Manchester UP, Manchester: 1980).

J. A. V. Chapple and Arthur Pollard (eds), *The Letters of Mrs Gaskell* (Manchester UP, Manchester: 1966; American issue, Harvard UP, Cambridge MA: 1967).

Christina Colvin (ed.), *Maria Edgeworth in France and Switzerland: Selections from the Edgeworth Family Letters* (Oxford UP, Oxford: 1979).

Christina Colvin (ed.), *Maria Edgeworth: Letters from England, 1813–1844* (Oxford UP, Oxford: 1971).

Peter Coveney, *The Image of Childhood. The Individual and Society: A Study of the Theme in English Literature*, rev. edn (Penguin, Baltimore: 1967).

F. J. Harvey Darton, *Children's Books in England: Five Centuries of Social Life*, 3rd edn, revised by Brian Alderson (Cambridge UP, Cambridge: 1982).

Patricia Demers and Gordon Moyles (eds), *From Instruction to Delight: An Anthology of Children's Literature to 1850* (Oxford UP, Toronto: 1982).

Charles de Moüy, from a signed article, *Revue Européenne* 17 (1 September 1861), pp. 138–64. Qtd. in Easson, pp. 489–504.

Angus Easson (ed.), *Elizabeth Gaskell: The Critical Heritage* (The Critical Heritage Series, Routledge, New York: 1991).

Maria Edgeworth and Richard Lovell Edgeworth, *Practical Education* (printed by George F. Hopkins, for self, and Brown & Stansbury; New York: 1801). First American edition. 2 vols.

Sarah Stickney Ellis, *The Mothers of England: Their Influence and Responsibility* (London: 1843; Research Publications, New Haven: 1975).

Willis J. Elwood and A. Félicité Tuxford (eds), *Some Manchester Doctors: A Biographical Collection to Mark the 150th Anniversary of the Manchester Medical Society, 1834–1984* (Manchester UP, Manchester: 1984).

John Forster, from an unsigned review of *Mary Barton*, *Examiner* (4 November 1848), pp. 708–9. Qtd. in Easson, pp. 67–70.

Elizabeth Cleghorn Gaskell, *'My Diary': The Early Years of My Daughter Marianne*, ed. Clement Shorter (1923).

Elizabeth Gaskell, *Mary Barton: A Tale of Manchester Life*, edited with an introduction by Stephen Gill (Penguin Classics, London: 1970; rpt. 1985).

Winifred Gérin, *Elizabeth Gaskell: A Biography* (Clarendon, Oxford: 1976).

Sandra M. Gilbert and Susan Gubar (eds), *The Norton Anthology of Literature by Women* (Norton, New York: 1985).

Christina Hardyment, *Dream Babies: Three Centuries of Good Advice on Child Care* (Harper, New York: 1983).

Augustus J. C. Hare, *The Years with Mother*, ed. M. Barnes (London: 1952).

Margaret Homans, *Bearing the Word: Language and Female Experience in Nineteenth-Century Women's Writing* (Chicago UP, Chicago: 1986).

Richard Hunter and Ida MacAlpine (eds), *Treatment of the Insane Without Mechanical Restraints*, by John Conolly (1856; rpt. Folkestone and London: 1973).

Mary V. Jackson, *Engines of Instruction, Mischief, and Magic: Children's Literature in England from Its Beginnings to 1839* (Nebraska UP, Lincoln, Nebraska: 1989).

Charles Kingsley on *Mary Barton*, from an unsigned review, *Fraser's Magazine* 39 (April 1849), pp. 417–32. Qtd. in Easson, pp. 152–5.

Elizabeth Langland, 'Nobody's angels: Domestic ideology and middle-class women in the Victorian novel', *PMLA* 107 (1992), pp. 290–304.

John Locke, *Some Thoughts Concerning Education*, ed. John W. Yolton and Jean S. Yolton (Clarendon, Oxford: 1989).

Edna Lyall, 'Mrs Gaskell', in *Women Novelists of Queen Victoria's Reign: A Book of Appreciations by Mrs Oliphant et al.* (Hurst and Blackett, London: 1897), pp. 117–45.

Harriet Mozley, *The Fairy Bower* (James Burns, London: 1841).

Mitzi Myers, 'Impeccable governesses, rational dames, and moral mothers: Mary Wollstonecraft and the female tradition in Georgian children's books', *Children's Literature* 14 (1986), pp. 31–59.

Mitzi Myers, 'Romancing the moral tale: Maria Edgeworth and the problematics of pedagogy', *Romanticism and Children's Literature in Nineteenth-Century England*, ed. James Holt McGavran, Jr. (Georgia UP, Athens, Georgia: 1991), pp. 96–128.

Linda Pollock, *A Lasting Relationship: Parents and Children Over Three Centuries* (New England UP, Hanover and London: 1987).

Hilary M. Schor, *Scheherezade in the Marketplace: Elizabeth Gaskell and the Victorian Novel* (Oxford UP, Oxford: 1992).

John Geoffrey Sharps, *Mrs Gaskell's Observation and Invention: A Study of Her Non-biographic Works* (Linden Press, London: 1970).

Alan Shelston, Letter to the author, 2 December 1992.

Patsy Stoneman, *Elizabeth Gaskell* (Indiana UP, Bloomington: 1987).

Karen Taylor, 'Blessing the house: Moral motherhood and the suppression of physical punishment', *Journal of Psychohistory* 15.1 (1987), pp. 431–54.

Mary F. Thwaite, *From Primer to Pleasure in Reading* (1st American edn; Horn Book, Boston: 1972).

Jenny Uglow, *Elizabeth Gaskell: A Habit of Stories* (Farrar, Straus, and Giroux, New York: 1993).

A. W. Ward (ed.), *The Works of Mrs. Gaskell*, Vols I and II, Knutsford edn (8 vols.; London: 1906).

Anita C. Wilson, 'Mother and writer: A study of Elizabeth Gaskell's diary', *The Gaskell Society Journal* 7 (1993), pp. 67–79.

Lynn Woodbury, 'Elizabeth Gaskell and the Victorian outsider: A study of "My Diary: The Early Years of My Daughter Marianne", *Mary Barton* and *Ruth*', *DAI* 44, p. 2479A (California UP, Santa Cruz: 1984).